THE COMPLETE GUIDE TO
BUGS AND INSECTS

An Imprint of Sterling Publishing
387 Park Avenue South
New York, NY 10016

Designed and edited by: Starry Dog Books Ltd

ISBN: 978-1-4351-4404-0 (print format)

A CIP record for this book is available from the Library of Congress.

For information about custom editions, special sales, and premium and
corporate purchases, please contact Sterling Special Sales at 800-805-5489
or specialsales@sterlingpublishing.com.

Manufactured in China
Lot #:
10 9 8 7 6 5 4 3 2 1
09/12

THE COMPLETE GUIDE TO
BUGS AND INSECTS

MELANIE BRIDGES

Sandy Creek
NEW YORK

CONTENTS

Words in **bold** are explained in the Glossary on page 136.

INTRODUCTION TO INSECTS

Did you know that a mosquito's wings beat 500 times a second, or that a spittlebug can jump 100 times higher than its own body length? There are more **insects** than any other type of creature on Earth. Spiders are not insects. They belong to a separate group of animals, called **arachnids**, which includes scorpions and ticks.

FREAKY FACT

To make honey, bees collect **nectar** from flowers. They spit it out in their hive, then dry it out with their wings.

Mosquitoes feed on the blood of other creatures, including humans. Their bites can spread diseases.

Making a home

Insects are good at **adapting** to different surroundings. Their small size means they can live in places that don't suit other creatures. They are found all over the world, and in all sorts of **habitats**—from deserts and mountains to **rainforests** and swamps. There are even a few insects in icy **Antarctica**!

Beetles that live in the Namib Desert "drink" the desert fog. Drops of water in the fog stick to the beetle's wings and run down into its mouth.

Tiny grains of pollen stick to a bee's body as it feeds and collects nectar from a flower.

Life on Earth

Insects that destroy **crops** or spread **disease** are thought of as pests. Some hurt us with their stings, but insects are also a very important part of life on Earth. They recycle dead plants and animals, help add goodness to soil, and pollinate plants.

WHAT ARE INSECTS?

Insects belong to a group of animals called **invertebrates.** These are creatures that do not have a backbone. Slugs, snails, and crabs belong to the same group, but insects are the only invertebrates that can fly. They live in all sorts of places, and eat almost every type of food— from plants and fish to wood and dung.

Silkworms are the caterpillars of the silk moth. Their cocoons are made from about 3,000 feet of very fine silk thread.

Really useful

Scientists study insects to find out more about how these fascinating creatures live, and how insects that threaten us can be controlled. Some insects provide us with useful products, such as honey, beeswax, **silk**, and dyes.

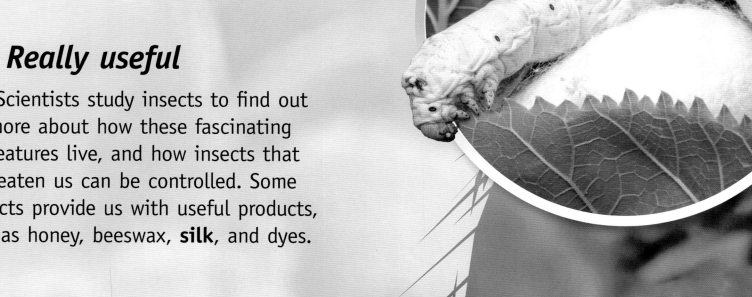

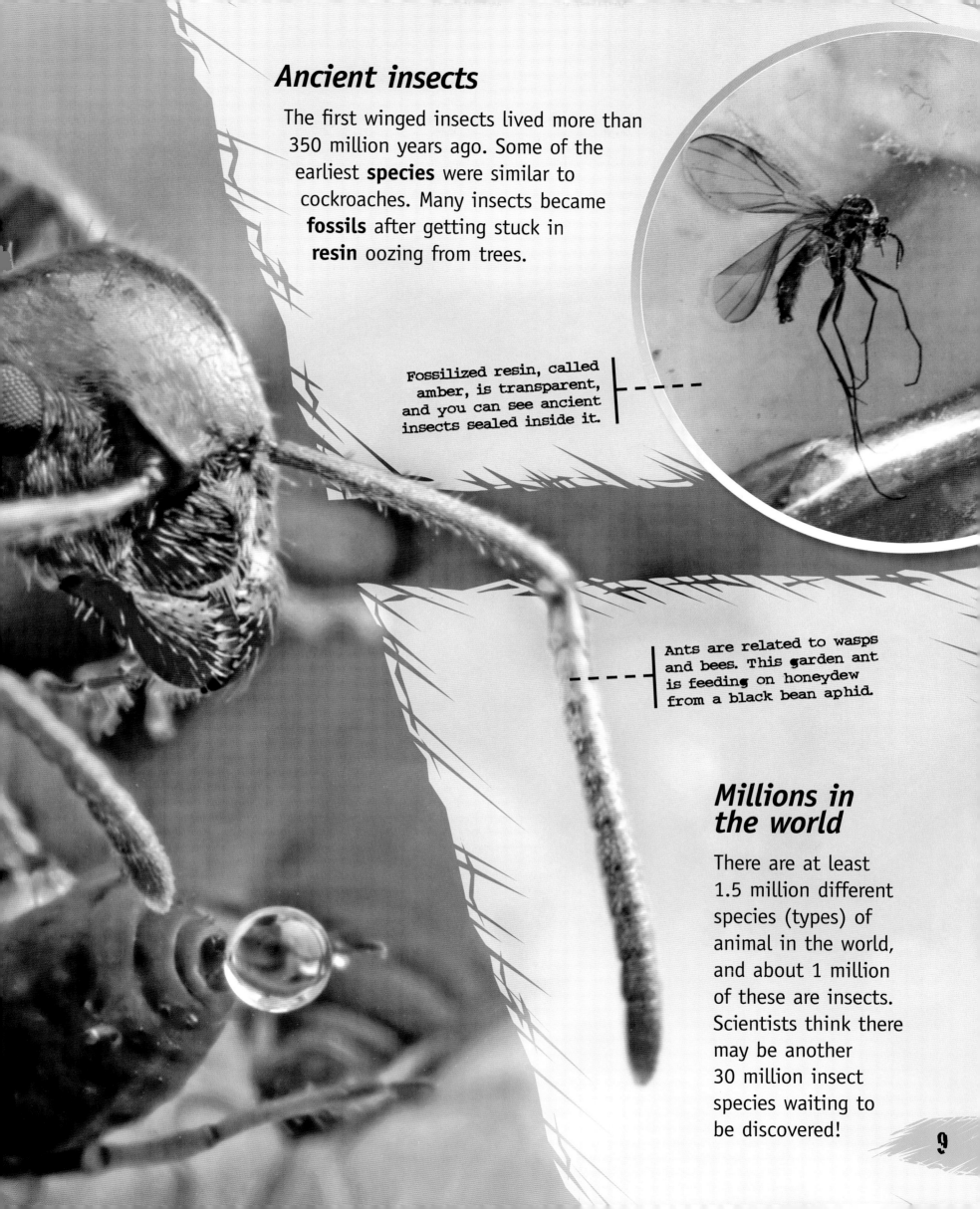

Ancient insects

The first winged insects lived more than 350 million years ago. Some of the earliest **species** were similar to cockroaches. Many insects became **fossils** after getting stuck in **resin** oozing from trees.

Fossilized resin, called amber, is transparent, and you can see ancient insects sealed inside it.

Ants are related to wasps and bees. This garden ant is feeding on honeydew from a black bean aphid.

Millions in the world

There are at least 1.5 million different species (types) of animal in the world, and about 1 million of these are insects. Scientists think there may be another 30 million insect species waiting to be discovered!

INSECT BODIES

Ground beetles use their strong jaws to attack and eat millipedes, slugs, and larvae, such as this mealworm.

Adult insects have six legs and a body with three parts—a head, **thorax** (middle section), and **abdomen** (end section). They also have two **antennae**, or feelers. Instead of having bones on the inside, they have a hard outer layer of skin that protects their soft bodies and **organs**, such as the heart.

Mouthparts

Insects have adapted to suit a wide range of different lifestyles and environments. Ground beetles, for example, are meat eaters, with large jaws that are perfect for cutting up **prey**. Mosquitoes prefer to suck up their food, so their mouthparts are shaped like a straw with a sharp tip. The mosquito pushes the tip into its victim's skin and feeds on the blood inside.

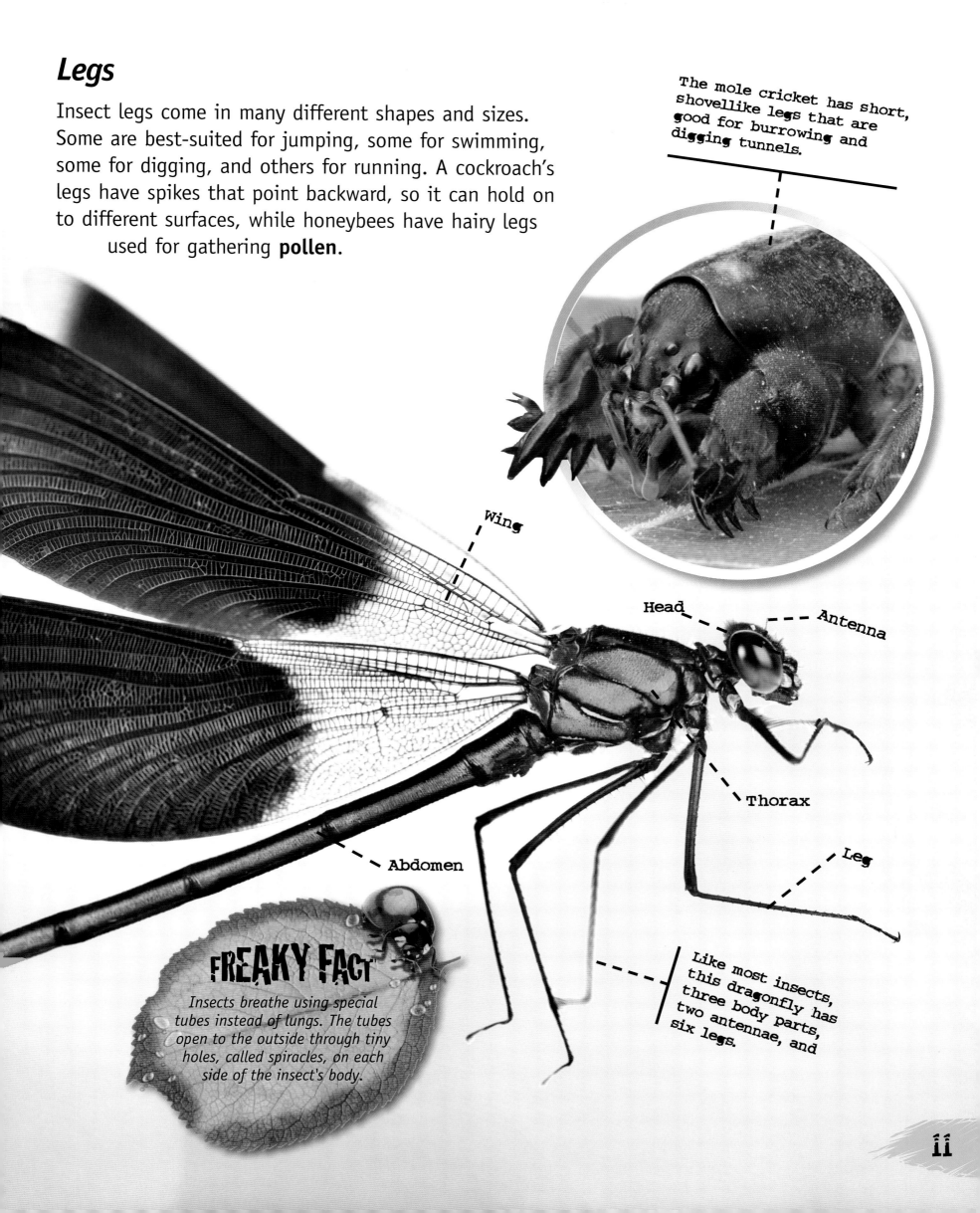

Legs

Insect legs come in many different shapes and sizes. Some are best-suited for jumping, some for swimming, some for digging, and others for running. A cockroach's legs have spikes that point backward, so it can hold on to different surfaces, while honeybees have hairy legs used for gathering **pollen**.

The mole cricket has short, shovellike legs that are good for burrowing and digging tunnels.

Wing

Head

Antenna

Thorax

Leg

Abdomen

FREAKY FACT

Insects breathe using special tubes instead of lungs. The tubes open to the outside through tiny holes, called spiracles, on each side of the insect's body.

Like most insects, this dragonfly has three body parts, two antennae, and six legs.

MORE INSECT BODIES

Insects use their antennae (feelers) to find out all about their surroundings. Tiny hairs on the antennae help the insect to sense smells, tastes, sounds, and movement. Some antennae have lots of branches, which make them even more sensitive.

Tiny scales add color and pattern to a butterfly's wings.

Wings

Most insects have two pairs of wings attached to their thorax. The wings are usually thin and filmy, but may also be covered with scales. Beetles have a hard pair of wings at the front, which covers and protects the pair behind. Some insects, such as flies, have only one pair of wings, and others, such as termites, do not develop wings at all.

A ladybug opens its hard, front wings and unfolds the thinner pair underneath, which it uses for flying.

This cicada has just molted for the last time. It climbs out of its old skin as a full-grown adult.

Growing up

All insects lay eggs. When the eggs hatch, the young may look like mini versions of the adults, or be very different. In order to grow to their full size, the young need to break out of their hard, outer skin. This is called molting, and it happens a few times during an insect's life. When it is ready to **molt**, the insect splits its old skin and wriggles out in a new skin.

13

TAKING FLIGHT

Insects were the first creatures to fly. This amazing skill helps them to escape from **predators**. It also means they can travel long distances to look for food or a mate.

FREAKY FACT

Painted lady butterflies fly across whole continents on their delicate wings to look for food or better weather.

Dragonflies were one of the first insects to take flight millions of years ago.

This crane fly's halteres are clearly visible just behind its wings.

Speedy fliers

Dragonflies are some of the speediest of all flying insects. They can fly at up to 34 miles per hour. If they flap all four wings at once, they can move quickly in a straight line. By flapping their front and back wings separately, they can also change direction, hover, stop in mid air, and even fly backward!

Counting beats

Dragonflies beat their wings about 25 times a second, whereas some small flies vibrate their wings 1,000 times a second. The sphinx moth beats its wings so fast that it can hover in midair to feed on the nectar inside a flower.

Haltere

The sphinx moth is sometimes mistaken for a bee—or even a hummingbird—because of the way it hovers while feeding.

A fly's halteres

Unlike other flying insects, flies have just one pair of wings. Tucked behind these, they have two small **halteres**, which look a bit like cotton swabs. These shake, or vibrate, as the fly zooms through the air, helping it to balance and change direction more easily.

15

DRAGONFLIES

Dragonflies live all over the world. There are more than 5,000 species altogether. The smallest is less than 1 inch across and the biggest can measure 6 inches.

All dragonflies have delicate wings, strong jaws, and large eyes, and they are expert hunters.

Catching prey

Colorful dragonflies are some of the fastest flying and most acrobatic of all insects. They dart and swoop in search of prey, such as flies and bees, which they generally catch in midair.

A dragonfly's legs are perfect for grabbing food, such as this bumblebee, or clinging onto plant stems.

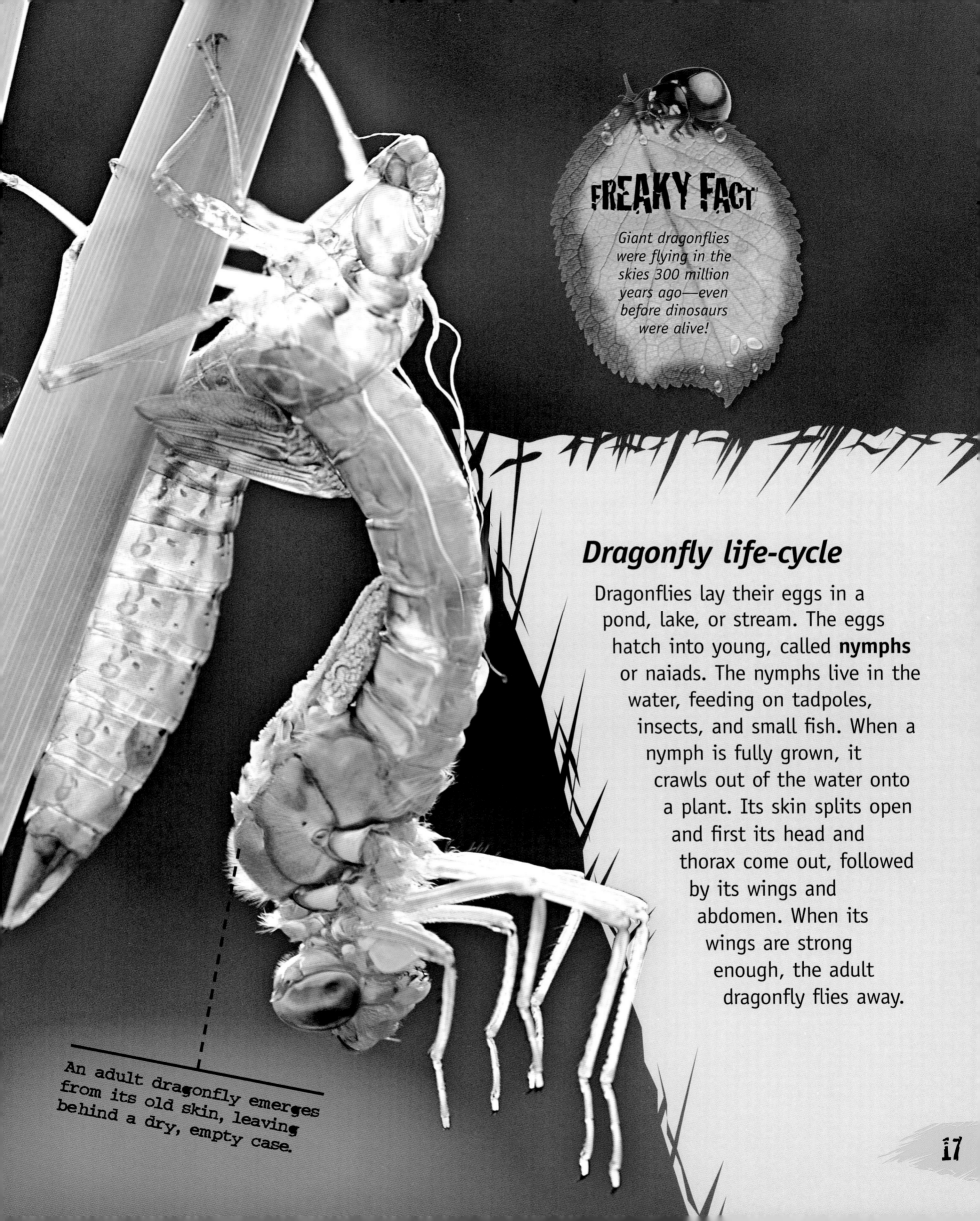

Giant dragonflies were flying in the skies 300 million years ago—even before dinosaurs were alive!

Dragonfly life-cycle

Dragonflies lay their eggs in a pond, lake, or stream. The eggs hatch into young, called **nymphs** or naiads. The nymphs live in the water, feeding on tadpoles, insects, and small fish. When a nymph is fully grown, it crawls out of the water onto a plant. Its skin splits open and first its head and thorax come out, followed by its wings and abdomen. When its wings are strong enough, the adult dragonfly flies away.

An adult dragonfly emerges from its old skin, leaving behind a dry, empty case.

MORE DRAGONFLIES

Dragonflies live in or near different types of water, from ponds and lakes to rivers, streams, and damp ditches.

Skimmers

Skimmers are named for the way the female skims over the surface of water and quickly dips her abdomen in to lay her eggs. Skimmers prefer warm, shallow, slow-moving water.

Biddies are also known as golden-ringed dragonflies because of the bright rings around their abdomen.

Biddies

Often seen near woodland streams, biddies have big eyes that almost meet in the middle. The head and thorax are covered in fine hairs, and the nymphs are hairy, too. The nymphs live at the bottom of streams, where they feed on tadpoles and water fleas.

Green darners

Green darners are among the biggest and fastest of all dragonflies. They are about 3 inches long, and live mostly in North America. A male darner allows females to visit his patch, but chases other males away. The adults feed on midges, mosquitoes, and other flying insects.

When green darners mate, the male chases the female, and places the end of his abdomen behind her head.

Like all skimmers, this flame, or firecracker, skimmer has a wide, flat body that is shorter than its wingspan.

FREAKY FACT

Dragonflies catch and eat other insects, but they also have to look out for birds, frogs, fish, and lizards, which eat them!

BRISTLETAILS AND MAYFLIES

Bristletails and mayflies are two of the most ancient groups of insects. Bristletails, such as silverfish and firebrats, have flat bodies and no wings. They are named for the three tails at the end of their body. These have a fringe of sensitive hairs, or bristles.

Silverfish are covered with shiny scales. Their flattened shape means they can squeeze into the tiniest of cracks.

Silverfish

Silverfish don't like light, and are often found under tree bark or in piles of rotting leaves. Many live inside houses, where they eat paper, glue, and spilled food. They can run fast, but cannot jump. Silverfish molt up to 30 times a year, even when they are full grown.

Mayfly larvae have similar tails to silverfish. They feed on algae and tiny plants.

Mayflies

Unlike bristletails, adult mayflies do have wings, but they are not strong fliers. The **larvae** live in water for over a year, molting many times before the wings develop. Once this happens, the adult mayfly lives for less than a day. This gives it just enough time to **mate** and lay eggs.

When resting, mayflies hold their wings upright like a butterfly.

FREAKY FACT

Just as their name suggests, firebrats love fire! They mostly live in warm places, such as near boilers, ovens, or fireplaces.

DAMSELFLIES

Damselflies belong to the same family as dragonflies. They have long, thin bodies and two pairs of transparent wings. Most species live near streams, rivers, ponds, or marshes, and they're found all over the world. They feed on insects, such as **aphids**, which they pick from plants.

FREAKY FACT

The biggest damselflies are found in South America. They can measure up to 7 inches long.

Damselfly nymphs breathe through three large gills at the end of their abdomen.

Damselflies hold their wings closed above their body when resting.

Colorful males

Male damselflies are often more colorful than females, and have bold markings on their legs and wings. Before **mating**, they fly or hover in front of the females to show off their bright colors.

A good place for eggs

The male damselfly looks for a good place for the female to lay her eggs. Then he attracts her to the place and chases other males away. The female lays her eggs through a special egg-laying tube in her body.

A female damselfly places her eggs inside a plant stem under water.

Damselfly nymphs

The nymphs that hatch from the eggs live in water, and catch small insects to eat. Some also feed on spiders. They move very quickly through the water, and are excellent hunters.

23

GRASSHOPPERS

There are more than 11,000 species of grasshopper, living everywhere from tropical jungles to deserts. All species have large heads, big eyes, and strong jaws. Their sight and hearing are excellent. Most have two pairs of wings. The narrow front pair covers and protects the wider back wings.

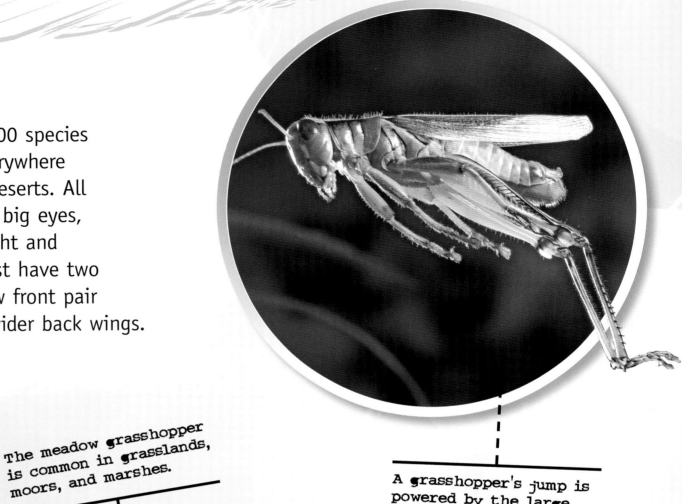

The meadow grasshopper is common in grasslands, moors, and marshes.

A grasshopper's jump is powered by the large muscles in its back legs.

FREAKY FACT

Grasshoppers are known for the scratchy, chirping noise they make by rubbing their front wings and back legs together.

Amazing jumpers

Like all insects, grasshoppers have three pairs of legs. Their back legs are much longer and stronger than the other two pairs, and are used for jumping. Some grasshoppers can jump up to 200 times the length of their own body.

Some grasshoppers cover their eggs with a frothy liquid. This mixes with soil and helps to protect the eggs.

Grasshopper life cycle

The female grasshopper lays 15 to 150 eggs in a row, a few inches underground. The eggs hatch into tiny young, called nymphs. As the nymphs grow, they molt five or six times before reaching adult size.

LONG-HORNED GRASSHOPPERS

There are two main groups of grasshoppers: long-horned and short-horned. Long-horned grasshoppers, such as katydids and crickets, have much longer antennae than their short-horned relatives.

False-leaf katydids can look like fresh, green leaves, dying brown ones, or a mixture of both.

Katydids

Katydids are named for the male's song, which sounds like the words "katy-did," or sometimes "katy-didn't!" They live all over the world. Katydids can grow to be 3 inches long. They feed on grass seeds, and many species come out only at night.

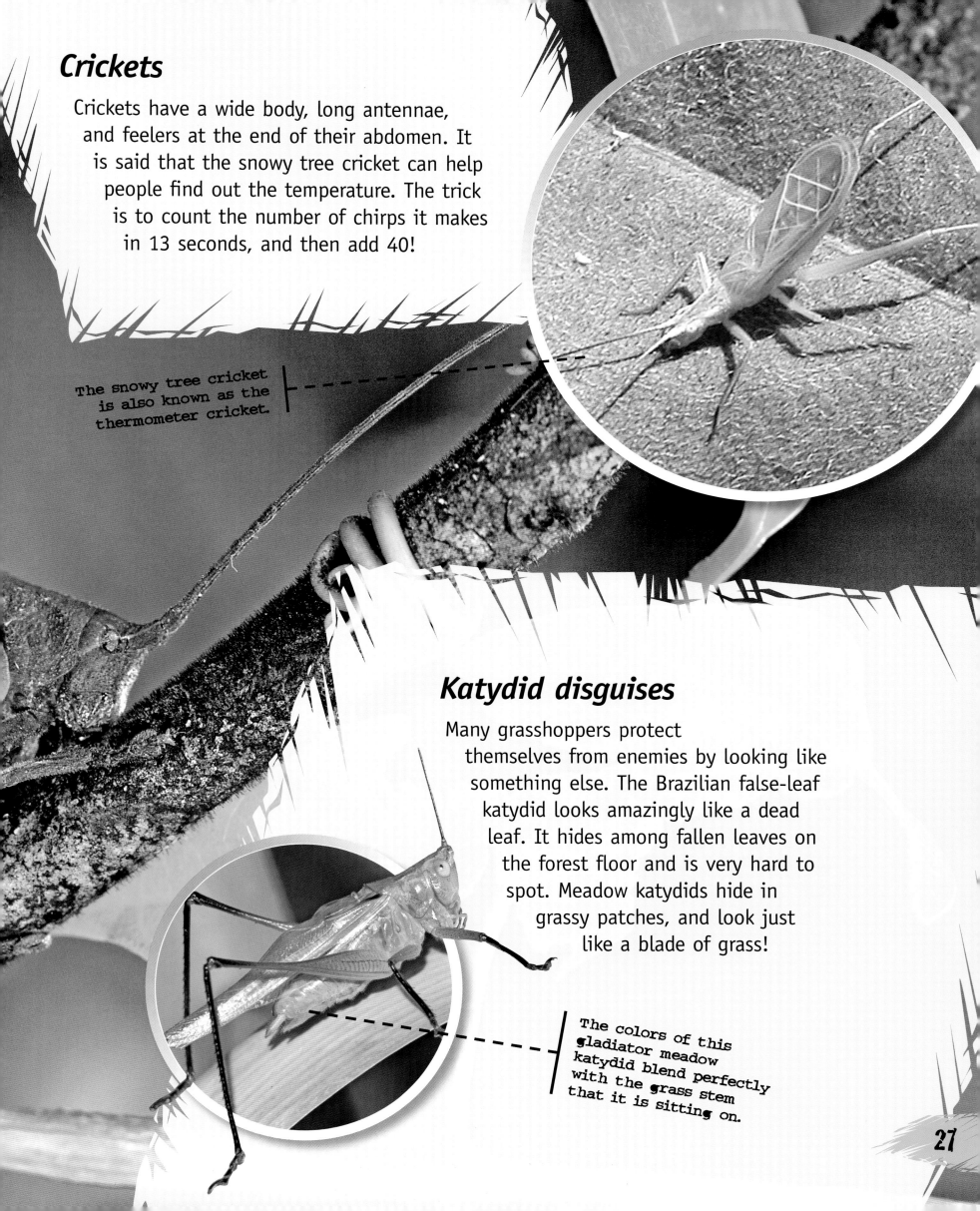

Crickets

Crickets have a wide body, long antennae, and feelers at the end of their abdomen. It is said that the snowy tree cricket can help people find out the temperature. The trick is to count the number of chirps it makes in 13 seconds, and then add 40!

The snowy tree cricket is also known as the thermometer cricket.

Katydid disguises

Many grasshoppers protect themselves from enemies by looking like something else. The Brazilian false-leaf katydid looks amazingly like a dead leaf. It hides among fallen leaves on the forest floor and is very hard to spot. Meadow katydids hide in grassy patches, and look just like a blade of grass!

The colors of this gladiator meadow katydid blend perfectly with the grass stem that it is sitting on.

SHORT-HORNED GRASSHOPPERS

Short-horned grasshoppers have short antennae, usually about half their body length. These grasshoppers are well-known for their rasping calls, which they make by rubbing rough patches on the back wings against the front wings.

FREAKY FACT

In some parts of the world, people cook and eat locusts as a tasty snack!

Spur-throated grasshoppers feed on grasses, leaves, fruit, flowers, and tree bark.

Spur-throated grasshoppers

These grasshoppers spend most of their lives among grass and other plants. To escape danger, they leap into the air and fly a little way before landing. The sudden flash of bright color on their wings alarms their enemies.

Desert locusts

Locusts are famous for causing serious damage to crops. When there is plenty of food around, they live and feed alone. But when food is hard to find, they gather together in huge **swarms** of up to 50 billion. The locusts swoop down onto fields of crops and feed until there is nothing left.

Locust swarms, such as this one in Africa, can be carried for hundreds of miles by the wind.

Young locusts change color from green to yellow and black

EARWIGS AND COCKROACHES

Cockroaches have existed for more than 350 million years. They live in many different habitats, from mountains to tropical rainforests. A few species live in buildings, and are considered pests. Earwigs feed on plants and flowers, and can also be pests. Their flat bodies make it easy for them to crawl into small hiding places.

American cockroach

This insect is found all over the world. It usually stays hidden during the day, and comes out at night to eat. It eats a wide range of things, including paper, hair, cloth, and almost anything that is rotting.

The American cockroach is attracted to sweet foods, such as apple.

Common earwig

The common earwig has short wings, a long, shiny body, and a forked tail. The female lays her eggs in a nest under a stone or log. Unusually for an insect, she stays near the nest to protect the eggs and lick them clean. She also looks after the young until they are able to feed themselves.

Earwigs use their pincers for sensing the environment, as well as for defense.

FREAKY FACT

If attacked, long-horned earwigs squirt out a nasty-smelling liquid from **glands** in their abdomen.

Madagascar hissing cockroach

When alarmed, this large cockroach makes a loud, hissing sound through breathing holes in its abdomen. Males also hiss when they are fighting each other. They usually live in forests. Some people keep them as pets.

The Madagascar hissing cockroach can grow up to 3 inches long.

MANTIDS

Mantids are some of the fiercest predators in the insect world. There are about 1,800 species, and most of them live in tropical areas. Their extra-long front legs are much stronger than their back legs. Mantids stretch them out at lightning speed to grab prey, which they almost never miss.

FREAKY FACT

Female praying mantids are bigger than males, and they often attack or even eat the male during mating.

The spiny flower mantis lives in southern and eastern Africa. It is named for the spines on the base of its abdomen.

Camouflage

Camouflage is very important for mantids when they're hunting. It helps them to stay hidden as they wait for prey to get close enough to catch. Most mantids are green or brown, so they can easily hide on leaves or twigs. Flower mantids, however, perch on flowers, and are colored to match them.

The praying mantis has sharp spikes on its legs. These help it to hold prey tightly.

Praying mantis

The praying mantis gets its name from its habit of sitting with its front legs folded, so it looks like a person praying. Mantids can turn their heads a long way so they can look back over their shoulders. This allows them to follow the movements of the prey they are about to attack.

TERMITE NESTS

Many insects have short lives, and don't need to make homes. But some insects make grand shelters and live together in groups. Termite nests can hold over 1 million termites. The nest protects them from enemies, and gives them a dark, warm, damp place to live. This is important because they can only survive in the open air for a few hours.

Some termite nests, such as this one in Cameroon, are shaped like a mushroom so that heavy rain runs off.

Termite towers

Some African termites make nests up to 25 feet tall. The termites mix mud with spit. When the mixture dries, it hardens. The main part of the nest is underground. It has chambers for the larvae and other chambers for storing food, as well as a special **cell** for the **queen**. The termites come and go from the nest through tunnels.

FREAKY FACT

Some termite nests have their own underground "garden," where the termites grow fungus to eat and feed to their young.

Tree nests

Some termites make their nests around tree branches. Inside is a maze of passages, with the queen termite in the middle. These termites also build covered paths along the branches and down the trunk to protect them as they come and go from the nest.

Tree nests are made from little pieces of wood mixed with termite spit.

The mud tower is a chimney that lets fresh air into the nest and old air out.

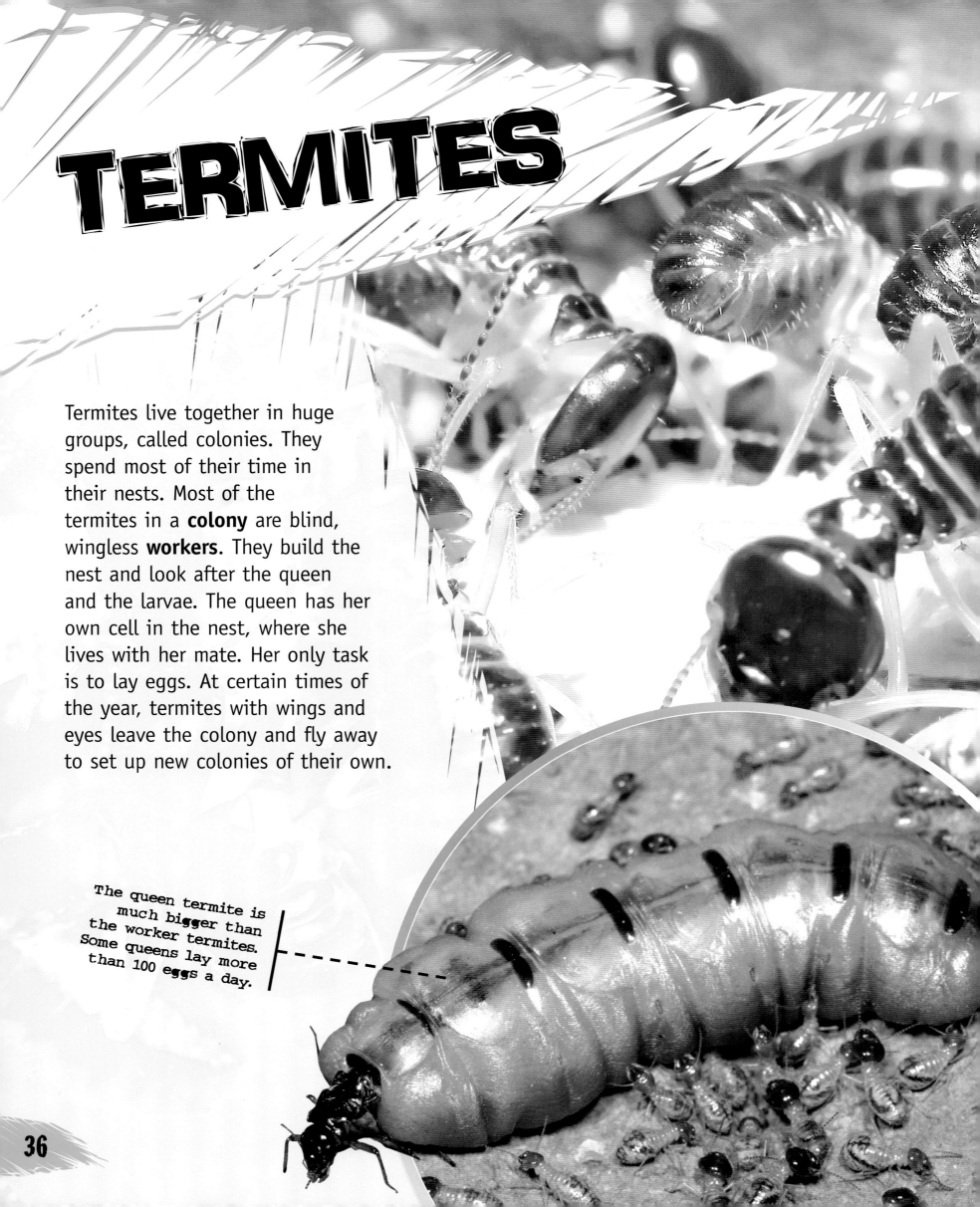

TERMITES

Termites live together in huge groups, called colonies. They spend most of their time in their nests. Most of the termites in a **colony** are blind, wingless **workers**. They build the nest and look after the queen and the larvae. The queen has her own cell in the nest, where she lives with her mate. Her only task is to lay eggs. At certain times of the year, termites with wings and eyes leave the colony and fly away to set up new colonies of their own.

The queen termite is much bigger than the worker termites. Some queens lay more than 100 eggs a day.

Eating wood

Many termite species feed on wood. They have special germs in their stomach that break down this tough food. Some species of wood-eating termite are thought of as a serious pest.

Wood-eating termites eat the wood of buildings, furniture, and stored timber.

FREAKY FACT

Termite colonies eat nonstop, 24 hours a day, 7 days a week!

These snouted harvester termite soldiers are guarding their mound nest while the workers are out collecting grass to eat.

Soldiers

Most termite colonies include soldier termites that defend the nest against attacks from enemies, such as ants. Some types of soldier termites have a bigger head and jaws than the workers. Others, such as the snouted termite, can spray a sticky, nasty-smelling liquid at their enemies.

37

LEAF INSECTS AND STICK INSECTS

Stick and leaf insects look amazingly like twigs and leaves. Their camouflage helps them to stay hidden from predators. There are about 3,000 species. Most of them live in tropical countries, where they eat plants and leaves.

During the day, stick insects cling to plants, but at night they move around, feeding on leaves.

Stick insects

With their thin green or brown bodies, stick insects look so like leafless twigs that birds and other predators find it hard to spot them. Some of them can change color to match the color of the leaves they are living in. Stick insects are also known as walking sticks.

Leaf insects

These amazing insects are shaped just like the leaves they live on. They even have similar vein patterns. Their legs are like leaves, too, and their eggs look like the seeds of the plant. As they walk, leaf insects often sway slightly, just like leaves in a breeze. Only male leaf insects can fly.

The ragged edges around this leaf insect's body look like the bite marks that you often see on real leaves.

39

STONEFLIES, BARKLICE, AND WEBSPINNERS

Stoneflies, barklice, and webspinners are three separate insect groups. Stoneflies are not true flies, and barklice are not lice at all!

Webspinner larvae are protected from predators by their silk tunnels.

Webspinners

Webspinners live in colonies, inside chambers and tunnels that they spin from silk. The tunnels connect their nest with food supplies, such as lichen, moss, and rotting leaves. Only the females and young feed. Males have short lives and do not eat.

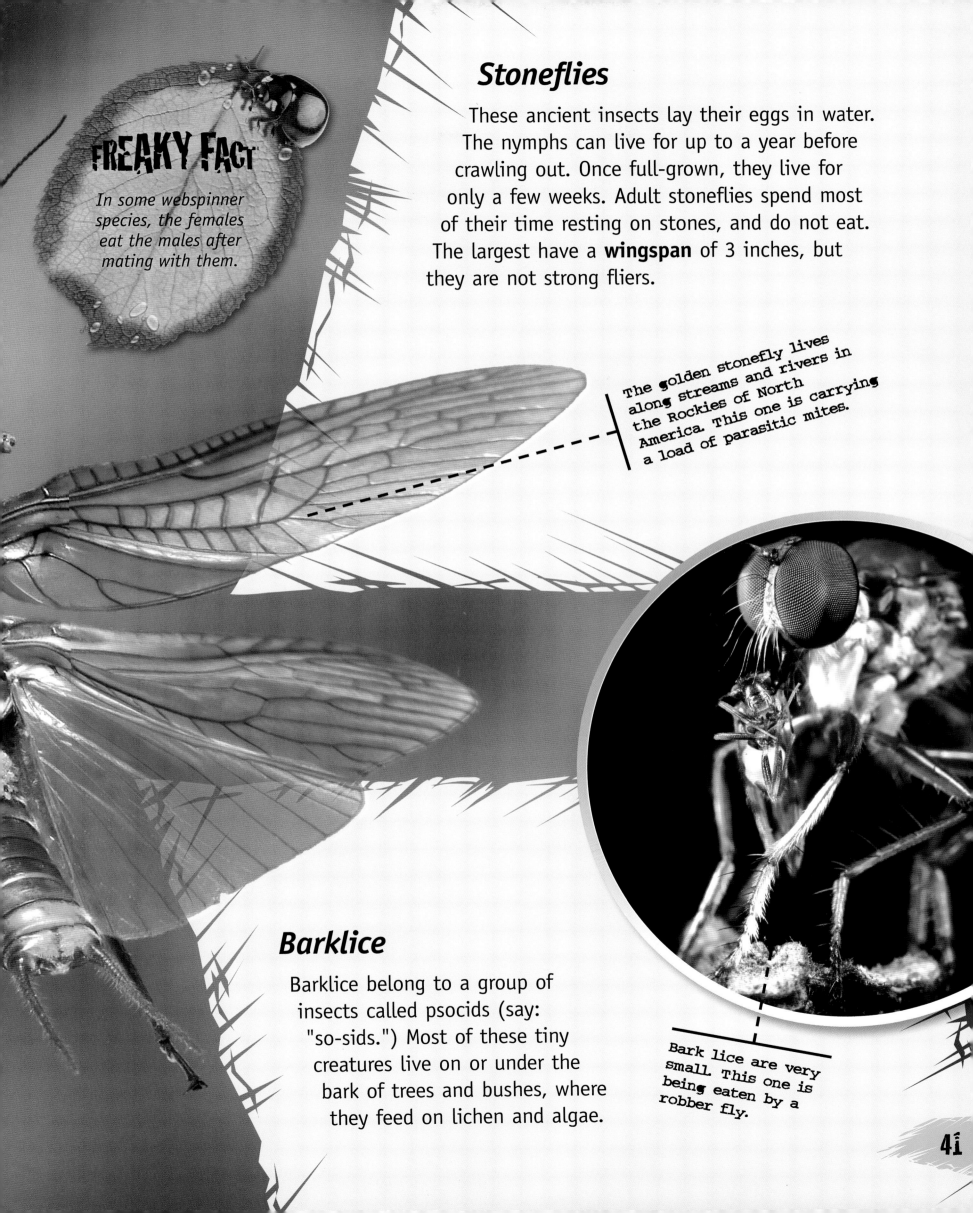

Stoneflies

These ancient insects lay their eggs in water. The nymphs can live for up to a year before crawling out. Once full-grown, they live for only a few weeks. Adult stoneflies spend most of their time resting on stones, and do not eat. The largest have a **wingspan** of 3 inches, but they are not strong fliers.

The golden stonefly lives along streams and rivers in the Rockies of North America. This one is carrying a load of parasitic mites.

Barklice

Barklice belong to a group of insects called psocids (say: "so-sids.") Most of these tiny creatures live on or under the bark of trees and bushes, where they feed on lichen and algae.

Bark lice are very small. This one is being eaten by a robber fly.

41

BUGS

Although "bug" is often used to describe insects in general, it is also an actual group of insects. Bugs range from 0.5 to 4.5 inches long.

Stinkbug eggs hatch after 1 to 3 weeks.

Bug life cycle

Most bugs lay eggs, but some, such as aphids, give birth to live young. A female bug lays her eggs on a plant or on the ground. The eggs hatch into nymphs, which look like tiny, wingless adults. The nymphs molt up to 6 times before they are full grown.

Mouthparts

The most important feature of a bug is its mouthparts. These are made to slice open food and suck up the liquid inside. Many bugs feed on plant juices, but some hunt other creatures. A few types, such as bedbugs, are parasites. They live on other creatures, including humans, and feed by piercing their skin and sucking their blood.

Soldier bugs help farmers to control pests by feeding on larvae and caterpillars that can damage crops.

MORE BUGS

There are about 90,000 species of true bugs. All have sucking mouthparts, which they can swing forward to reach a greater range of foods.

Plantbugs

Plantbugs are the biggest family of true bugs. They live all over the world. Most of them feed on leaves, seeds, and fruit, but some are serious pests, eating crops such as cotton and tea.

Plantbugs pierce leaves and suck out the juices.

Assassin bugs

Fierce-looking assassin bugs attack and kill other insects, such as **caterpillars**, beetles, bees, and other bugs. Once they have caught their prey, they inject it with spit. This stops the insect from moving, and the assassin then sucks up all of its victim's body juices.

44

Stinkbugs

These bugs are named for the nasty-smelling liquid that they spray over attackers. Most predators run away as soon as they smell it. A stinkbug's mouthparts are inside its beak-shaped snout. It uses them to stab plants so that it can suck up the **sap** inside.

The smelly liquid that a stinkbug uses to warn off predators comes from two stink organs underneath its body.

An assassin bug uses its long mouthparts to inject venom into a stink or shield bug.

LICE
AND THRIPS

Lice are small, wingless insects that live as parasites on other creatures. There are two main types: sucking lice and chewing lice. Thrips are related to lice, but are not parasites.

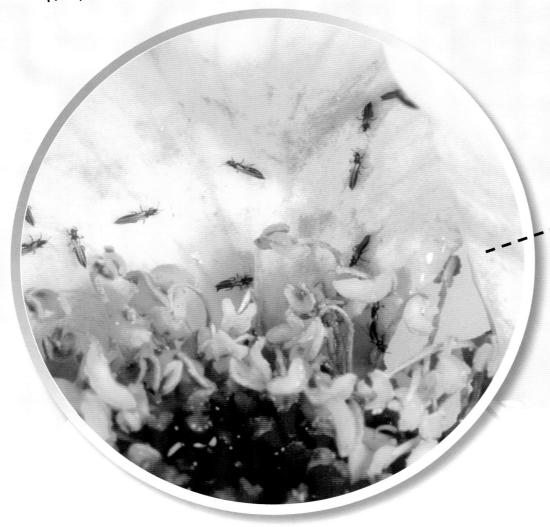

Rose thrips feed and lay their eggs deep inside a rosebud or flower.

Thrips

There are as many as 5,000 species of thrips. Some are pests of particular plants or crops. These tiny bugs pierce leaves or flowers, and suck up the plant juices.

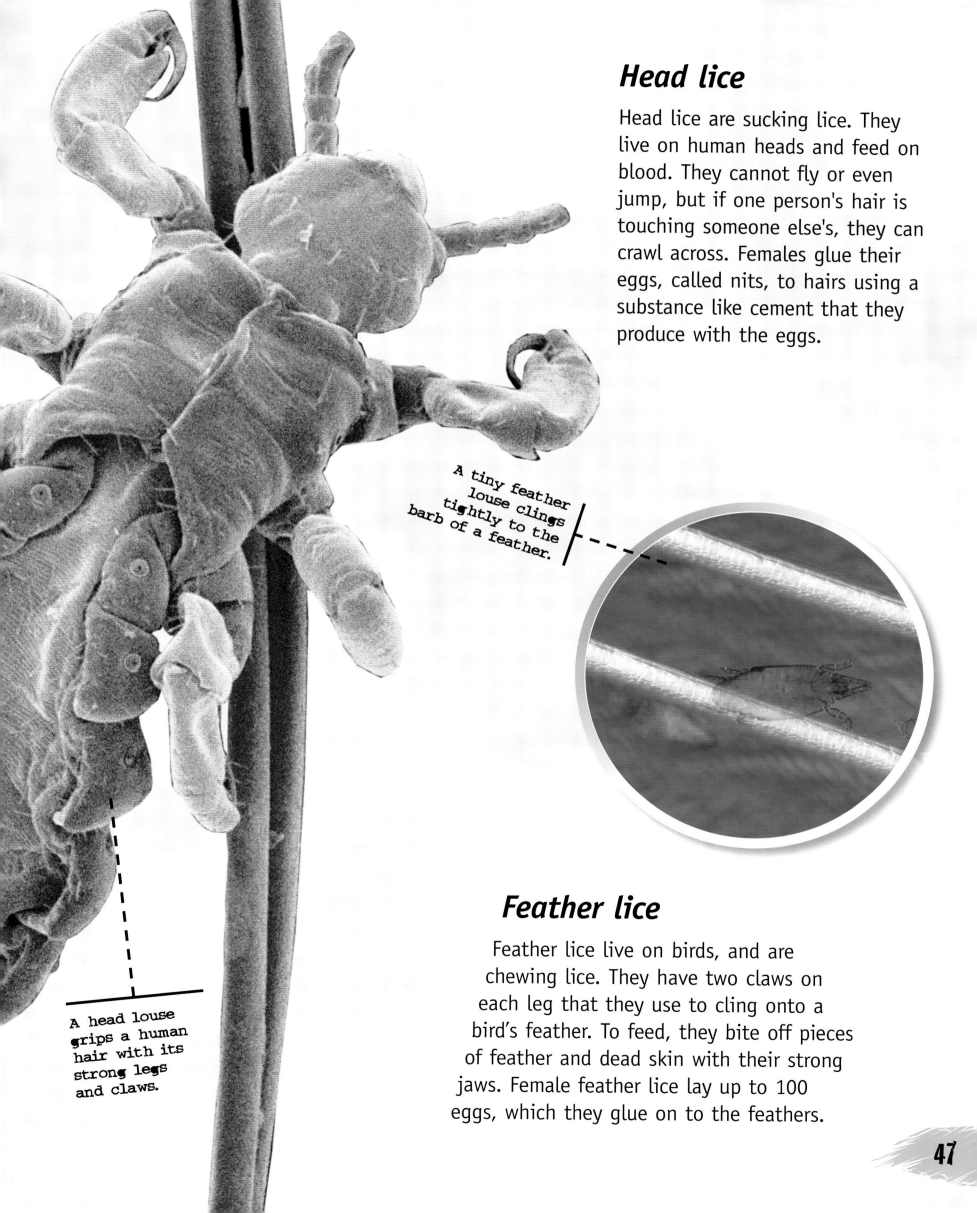

Head lice

Head lice are sucking lice. They live on human heads and feed on blood. They cannot fly or even jump, but if one person's hair is touching someone else's, they can crawl across. Females glue their eggs, called nits, to hairs using a substance like cement that they produce with the eggs.

A tiny feather louse clings tightly to the barb of a feather.

A head louse grips a human hair with its strong legs and claws.

Feather lice

Feather lice live on birds, and are chewing lice. They have two claws on each leg that they use to cling onto a bird's feather. To feed, they bite off pieces of feather and dead skin with their strong jaws. Female feather lice lay up to 100 eggs, which they glue on to the feathers.

WATER BUGS

More than 2,000 species of true bug live in ponds, streams, and lakes. Some of them are so light that they can run on the surface of the water without getting wet. Others live and hunt for food underwater and only come to the surface every so often to breathe.

FREAKY FACT

Giant water bugs can grow to be more than 4 inches long. Their prey includes fish and even frogs!

Water boatmen use their front legs for eating and collecting food, and the other two pairs for swimming.

Water boatmen

Unlike other water bugs, these soft-bodied insects are not predators. Instead, they feed on tiny plants and algae. Their back legs are shaped like oars and covered in hairs. This helps them to push their way through the water more easily.

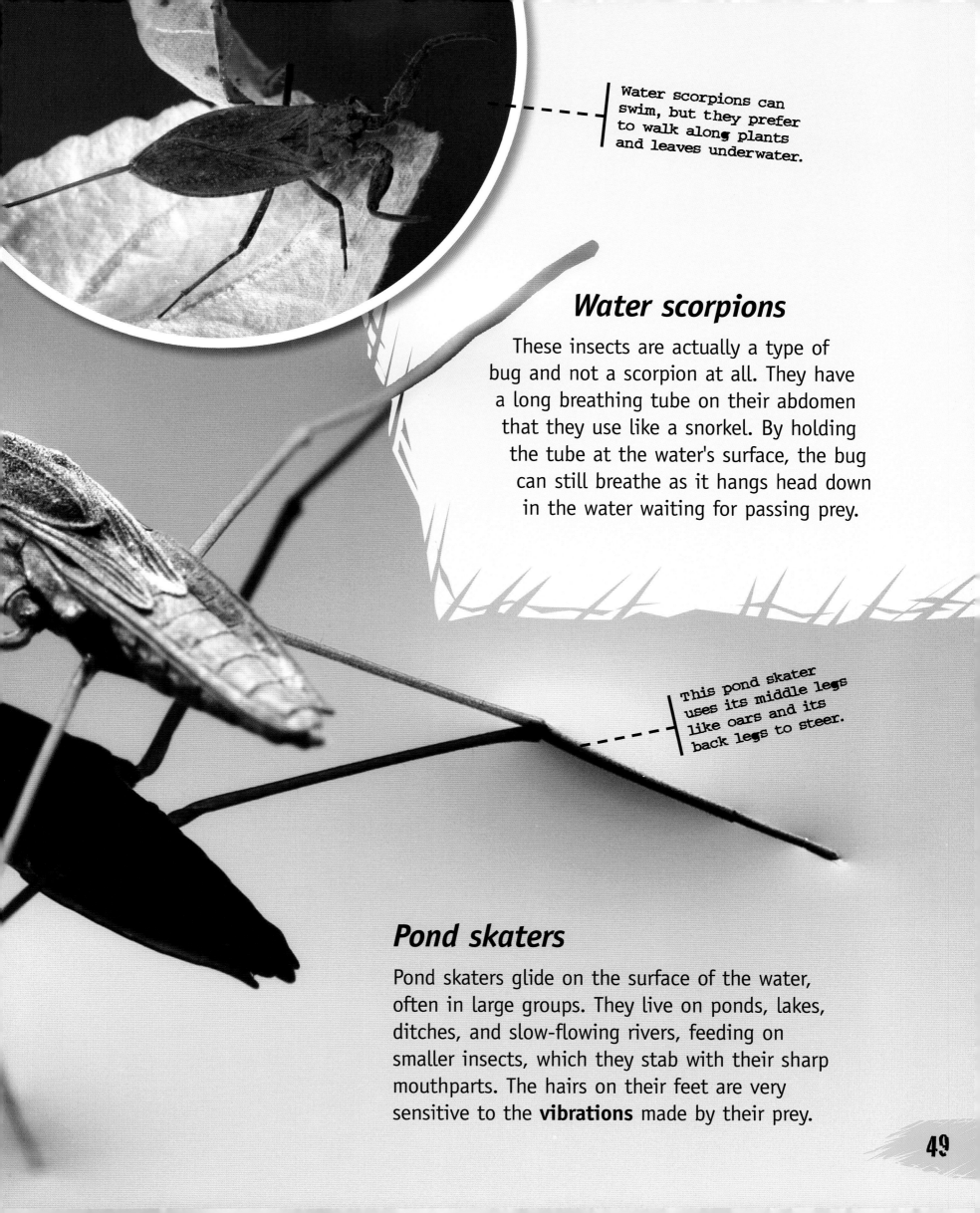

Water scorpions can swim, but they prefer to walk along plants and leaves underwater.

Water scorpions

These insects are actually a type of bug and not a scorpion at all. They have a long breathing tube on their abdomen that they use like a snorkel. By holding the tube at the water's surface, the bug can still breathe as it hangs head down in the water waiting for passing prey.

This pond skater uses its middle legs like oars and its back legs to steer.

Pond skaters

Pond skaters glide on the surface of the water, often in large groups. They live on ponds, lakes, ditches, and slow-flowing rivers, feeding on smaller insects, which they stab with their sharp mouthparts. The hairs on their feet are very sensitive to the **vibrations** made by their prey.

STAYING HIDDEN

All sorts of animals eat insects, so the insects need to find ways of protecting themselves. For many, the best way is to stay hidden. Some live under stones or leaves, but others are colored or shaped in a way that helps them to blend in with their surroundings. This is called camouflage. It makes the insects hard for other creatures to spot.

With its patchy coloring and straight body, it's hard to tell this geometrid caterpillar from the real twig.

50

Insect mimics

Some types of insect look just like leaves or twigs, and others are colored like bark or moss. The flower mantis looks like flower petals. As well as helping to camouflage it from predators, this also attracts prey. Its disguise is so good that flower-feeding insects come to investigate. As soon as they get close enough, the mantis catches and eats them.

Orchid mantids are black and orange when they first hatch, but they grow to look like beautiful orchid flowers.

Masters of disguise

Some caterpillars are experts at disguise. The geometrid caterpillar has a pair of grippers at the end of its body that it uses to hold on to a twig. Then it stretches out its body so that it looks just like another twig.

CICADAS, TREEHOPPERS, AND LEAFHOPPERS

This group of bugs includes a huge and varied range of insects. They range from tiny leafhoppers to giant cicadas.

A treehopper mother in Ecuador guards her newly hatched nymphs.

Treehoppers

Most treehoppers have a pointed section like a thorn on top of their body, and they are sometimes known as thorn bugs. Many types of treehopper are brightly colored, especially those that live in warm countries. They feed on sap from trees and other plants.

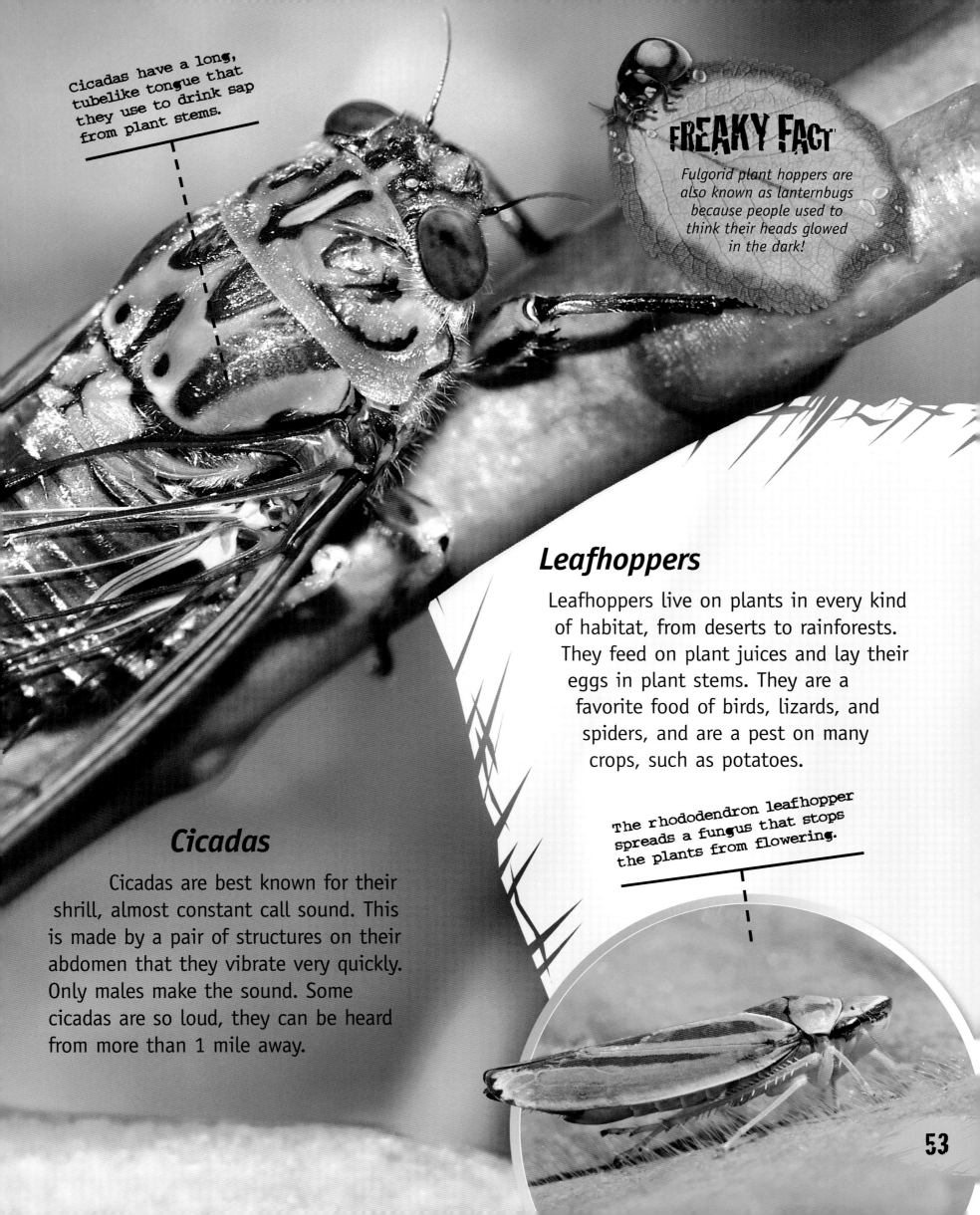

Cicadas have a long, tubelike tongue that they use to drink sap from plant stems.

Leafhoppers

Leafhoppers live on plants in every kind of habitat, from deserts to rainforests. They feed on plant juices and lay their eggs in plant stems. They are a favorite food of birds, lizards, and spiders, and are a pest on many crops, such as potatoes.

The rhododendron leafhopper spreads a fungus that stops the plants from flowering.

Cicadas

Cicadas are best known for their shrill, almost constant call sound. This is made by a pair of structures on their abdomen that they vibrate very quickly. Only males make the sound. Some cicadas are so loud, they can be heard from more than 1 mile away.

53

APHIDS
AND SCALE INSECTS

Aphids produce a sweet, sticky liquid, called honeydew, that ants eat. In return, the ants protect the aphids.

Aphids and scale insects are tiny, but can be serious pests. They feed on plant juices, often in large numbers on one plant.

Fine strings of wax help to hide this woolly alder aphid (a plant louse) from predators.

Jumping plant lice

These lice look like tiny cicadas. They jump as they move around plants feeding on their juices. Some hide themselves in clouds of a waxy substance that oozes out from below their tail.

Cottony cushion scale insects

These insects feed on the sap of citrus leaves. They are mostly found in tropical countries and greenhouses. The female has no wings. Her body is orange, yellow, or brown, and is often completely covered by white wax. She has a large, fluted egg case at the end of her body, which holds about 1,000 red eggs.

FREAKY FACT

Many scale insects are covered in a kind of wax that people use to make varnish and dyes.

A cottony cushion scale adult fixes itself to a plant and stays there until it dies. Its tiny nymphs are able to move around.

BEETLES

More than a quarter of a million beetle species have been discovered so far, and new ones are being found all the time. Beetles live almost everywhere, from tropical rainforests to deserts. Some are so small you can hardly see them. Others, such as the Goliath beetle, are among the largest of all insects.

FREAKY FACT

Dung beetles were introduced to Australia to eat up some of the dung produced by the millions of cattle in the country.

To fly, beetles, such as this cockchafer, open their front wings and unfold the back pair.

Protected wings

Beetles have two pairs of wings—one at the front and one at the back. The front wings are thick and hard. They cover and protect the back wings, which are more fragile.

The Goliath beetle can grow up to 4 inches long!

Beetle life cycle

A beetle lays its eggs in the ground, in wood, or on plants. Each egg hatches into a **larva**, also known as a grub. The larva feeds and grows, molting several times. When it is full grown, it stops eating and turns into a **pupa**, wrapped in a silky **cocoon**. Inside the cocoon, the pupa turns into a beetle. It eventually emerges as an adult beetle with wings.

The scarlet lily beetle covers her eggs with a thick, brown liquid to protect them from predators and the sun.

PLANT-EATING BEETLES

Many beetles eat plants. One family, the weevils, is the largest of all beetle families. It has more than 40,000 species, which live all over the world.

Boll weevils

This little beetle uses its long snout to make holes in the seedpods, or bolls, of the cotton plant. It eats the bolls and the buds. The female lays her eggs in the bolls. When they hatch, the larvae eat the seeds and destroy the plant.

A boll weevil sits on a damaged cotton boll

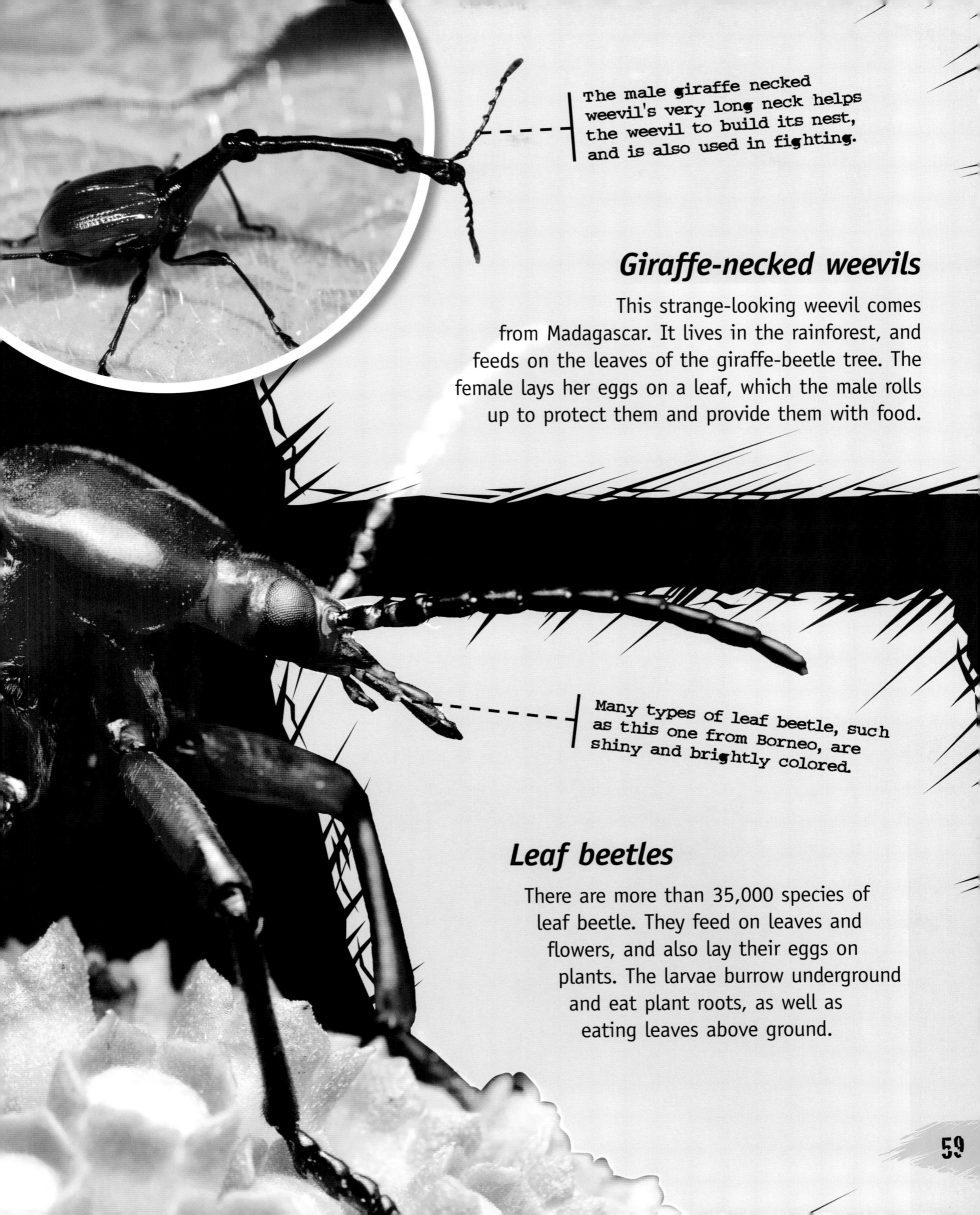

The male giraffe necked weevil's very long neck helps the weevil to build its nest, and is also used in fighting.

Giraffe-necked weevils

This strange-looking weevil comes from Madagascar. It lives in the rainforest, and feeds on the leaves of the giraffe-beetle tree. The female lays her eggs on a leaf, which the male rolls up to protect them and provide them with food.

Many types of leaf beetle, such as this one from Borneo, are shiny and brightly colored.

Leaf beetles

There are more than 35,000 species of leaf beetle. They feed on leaves and flowers, and also lay their eggs on plants. The larvae burrow underground and eat plant roots, as well as eating leaves above ground.

WOOD-EATING BEETLES

The larvae of many wood-eating beetles feed on dead and rotting trees. Others feed on live trees, furniture, and the wooden beams in houses.

Stag beetles

Male stag beetles have enormous jaws that look like the antlers of a stag deer. Like stags, they fight each other over females. Females lay their eggs in logs or dead tree stumps, and the larvae feed on juices from the rotting wood. The adults mostly feed on tree sap.

When stag beetles fight, the beetle with the largest jaws usually wins.

FREAKY FACT

It can take a stag beetle larva 5 years of munching on rotten wood before it becomes a full-grown adult.

Longhorn beetle

Some wood-eaters, such as longhorn beetles, cause a lot of damage and are a serious pest. They lay their eggs in trees, and the larvae tunnel into the wood.

Longhorn beetles use their long antennae to feel what is in front, around, and behind them.

A deathwatch beetle chews its way in and out of wood, leaving behind holes and piles of sawdust.

Deathwatch beetle

The deathwatch beetle bangs its head against wood to attract a mate. People used to think the tapping sound was a warning of death because they often heard it in the hushed room where a person was dying. The female lays her eggs in wood, and the larvae tunnel into it as they feed.

TIGER, WATER, AND GROUND BEETLES

Beetles have strong, chewing mouthparts. They use them to feed on many different types of food, both on land and in water.

Water beetles

Water beetles are predators. They include diving beetles, which live in ponds and lakes, where they catch prey much bigger than themselves. Diving beetles swim by moving their long, fringed back legs like oars.

When it dives, a diving beetle traps air under its wing cases to help it breathe underwater.

Tiger beetles

Tiger beetles are a large group of beetles known for being aggressive hunters. Like tigers, they move very quickly on their long legs to catch their prey. They are often brightly colored and shine like metal.

FREAKY FACT

The larvae of diving beetles are predators, just like the adults. They are sometimes known as water tigers.

If attacked, the caterpillar hunter gives off a nasty-smelling liquid that can cause blisters on human skin.

Tiger beetles have strong jaws for gripping onto their victims.

Ground beetles

Ground beetles live in gardens, fields, and woodlands all over the world. Some feed on plants, but most eat other insects. The large, shiny caterpillar hunter belongs to this family. Its main prey is caterpillars, which it will chase up trees.

63

SCARAB BEETLES

The scarab family includes some of the biggest of all beetles, such as the rhinoceros beetle. Many are very colorful and have unusual antennae that they can spread out to help them sense smells. Some feed on plants, and others eat dung or rotting animals.

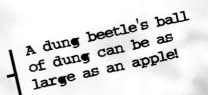

A dung beetle's ball of dung can be as large as an apple!

Dung beetles

This group of scarab beetles feeds on animal dung. The beetle rolls a lump of dung into a large ball, buries itself with the ball, and then eats it. Females lay their eggs in the middle of a dung ball, and when the larvae hatch, they feed on the dung.

Rhinoceros beetle

This amazing beetle is one of the largest insects in the world. The male's huge horns make up about half its length. It uses them to fight other males over food or to win a mate. Females are smaller and have no horns.

Although rhinoceros beetles look fierce, they are not predators. They eat only rotting plants.

This burying beetle is recycling a dead rat by feeding it to its larvae.

Burying beetles

Burying beetles feed on animals that are already dead. This is an important form of recycling. These flat-bodied beetles crawl underneath a small, dead animal, such as a bird or mouse, and then dig under the body until it sinks into the ground. The female then lays her eggs on the dead body, and later the young beetles feed on the rotting animal.

BLISTER BEETLES, LADYBUGS, AND ROVE BEETLES

These beetle families contain large numbers of species, and they live nearly all over the world.

Ladybugs

Ladybugs are some of the best-known of all beetles. They have a round, shiny body that is easy to recognize. Many have red or orange wing covers with black spots, but some are a different color and some have no spots at all. A ladybug's bright color warns its enemies that it tastes nasty and may be poisonous.

If a blister beetle is disturbed, it produces a smelly, oily liquid from its body.

Ladybugs mainly eat aphids, which are often protected by ants.

FREAKY FACT

People sometimes use the oily liquid from a blister beetle to help get rid of warts on their skin.

66

Blister beetles

Blister beetles, also known as oil beetles, usually live on flowers. In some species, the females lay as many as 10,000 eggs in May or June. Some blister beetle larvae attach themselves to a bee and get carried back to the bee's nest, where they feed on bee larvae, eggs, and stores of pollen.

If threatened, a rove beetle curls up to show off the yellow stripes on its abdomen that make it look like a wasp.

Rove beetles

There are about 45,000 species of rove beetle. Most have a long body and short **wing cases**. When disturbed, they arch the back end of their body like a scorpion. Both the adults and larvae prey on insects and worms.

67

GLOWING INSECTS

Some insects can glow in the dark. They use special chemicals inside their body to make a natural light. This is used to attract mates, trap prey, or keep attackers away.

Each thread is a trap made by the fungus gnat to catch its prey.

Fungus gnat

Four **fungus** gnat species in New Zealand and Australia live in caves and other dark, damp places. From their nests, the larvae hang sticky silk threads covered in droplets of glue. When they wave their glowing tail, midges, moths, and other insects are attracted to the light and get caught in the traps.

Fireflies

Fireflies, also known as glowworms, are a type of beetle that can produce a yellowish-green light from the end of their abdomen. Each species of firefly flashes its light in a particular pattern to attract mates of its own kind.

A male Japanese firefly lights up at dusk. Fireflies can make their light brigher or dimmer, and can shut it off.

FREAKY FACT

Some fireflies use their lights to warn enemies that they taste nasty and should be left alone.

Females of the common glowworm are twice the size of the males and do not have wings.

BEES

Bees belong to the same group of insects as wasps and ants. All three have a narrow "waist" section at the front of their abdomen. Bees have chewing mouthparts and a long tongue for sucking up liquids, such as nectar from flowers. Many bees live in large groups, or colonies, but some live on their own.

Bumblebees, such as this buff-tailed bumblebee, are important plant pollinators.

Bumblebees

There are about 250 species of bumblebee. They are usually black with some yellow markings, and have large, hairy bodies. Queen bumblebees can be up to 1 inch long, but worker bees are smaller. They live in small, underground colonies. Only the queen survives through the winter.

Carpenter bees

The female carpenter bee chews a tunnel-shaped nest in wood. She makes a row of cells inside the tunnel and fills each one with food. She then lays one egg in each cell. When the larvae hatch, they feed on the pollen and nectar in their cell. The queen bee stays nearby to guard the nest.

Most carpenter bees have a shiny abdomen, unlike hairy bumblebees.

In India and Southeast Asia, people gather honey from the combs of giant honeybees, even though the bees are aggressive.

Giant honeybees

These large bees make nests that hang from a tree, cave, or cliff. They are very fierce and attack any creature or person who tries to disturb their colony.

MORE BEES

Many types of bee live alone. These **solitary** bees feed on nectar and gather pollen to feed their young.

Red mason bee

The red mason bee nests in a hole in a plant stem, an old wall, or a fence post. Once the female has found a hole she likes, she stores some pollen inside, and lays an egg. She then seals the hole with a lid of mud to keep the egg safe.

A female red mason bee enters her nest in an old wall, carrying pollen for her food store.

Mining and plasterer bees

Mining bees dig their nest in the ground. Each bee has its own nest, but lots of them may live close together. Plasterer bees dig similar tunnels, which they line with a liquid from their abdomen that makes the tunnels waterproof.

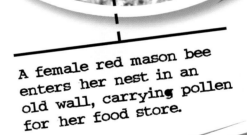

The tawny mining bee's nest is a vertical shaft with cells branching off it.

Leafcutter bees

These bees cut round pieces from leaves with their strong, scissorlike jaws and use them to line the cells of their nest, where they lay their eggs. Some leafcutter bees are parasites. They break into other leafcutters' nests and lay their eggs there. When the larvae hatch, they kill the young already in the nest and eat all the food.

A leafcutter bee carries a piece of leaf back to its nest. It lines each cell in its nest with 15 to 20 pieces of leaf.

FREAKY FACT

Stingless bees cannot sting, but they do have strong jaws that they use to protect themselves by biting attackers.

MAKING HONEY

Honeybees pollinate many food crops and make honey and wax, which farmers sell for millions of dollars each year. Thousands of honeybees can live in a single colony.

These female workers are looking after the larvae in their cells in a hive.

Worker bees

All worker bees are female. They leave the nest to look for pollen and nectar. When they come back, the other workers gather around to collect the food. They store it in special cells inside the nest. These are built from wax, which is made in tiny organs underneath the bee's abdomen. The bees squeeze the wax with their mouthparts until it is soft enough to use for building.

Drones and queens

Male bees, called **drones**, are only born at certain times of year, ready to mate with new queens. Each colony has a queen. She is bigger than the other bees and lays all the eggs in the colony.

Drone

The queen bee, here marked with a white dot, is laying eggs in queen cups.

A worker bee's tools

A worker bee has long hairs on each front leg that it uses to remove pollen from its body. On its middle legs it has fringes of hair for removing pollen from its front legs, and a spike for collecting wax from its abdomen. On each back leg it has a pollen sac lined with hairs, where pollen is carried.

This worker bee is drinking sweet nectar, which becomes honey when the water in it evaporates (dries off).

75

WASPS

Wasps sometimes seem annoying to humans, but they're actually very useful. They feed their young on insects, such as caterpillars and aphids, which can damage plants.

FREAKY FACT

In Japan, every year people die from the sting of the Asian giant hornet, which grows up to 2 inches long.

Adult wasps have strong jaws for biting into soft, sweet fruit.

European hornet

This large insect measures up to 1.25 inches long. It lives in colonies, in a nest built from a papery material that it makes by chewing up plants. The nest is usually in a tree or old building.

A European hornet adult feeds on a bee that it has caught.

Spider wasps

The female spider wasp catches spiders to feed her young. She **paralyzes** the spider with her sting, and places her prey in a section of her nest with an egg. She then seals the section with mud. When the wasp larva hatches, it eats the spider.

The spider is still alive when the spider wasp seals it in her nest for the larvae to eat.

Yellow jackets

Common wasps are also known as yellow jackets. Like most wasps, they have a sting at the end of their body. This is shaped like a pointed tube, and is joined to a bag full of poison, or **venom**. The wasp uses its sting to attack prey and protect itself from enemies, including humans. After stinging, it can pull its sting out and use it again.

WASPS' NESTS

Wasps are some of the most skilled builders in the insect world. Some are solitary—they make a nest, where they live on their own until their eggs hatch. Others work together in big groups, or colonies, to build a large nest from mud or chewed wood pulp.

The papery material that paper wasps use to make their nest is waterproof.

Paper wasps

The paper wasp starts its nest alone. A female makes a few papery pockets from chewed up wood mixed with her own spit. She then lays an egg in each pocket. Once her young are full grown, they become workers, and she becomes a queen. The workers make the nest bigger and the queen lays more eggs. In the fall, most wasps in the colony die, leaving behind just one young queen.

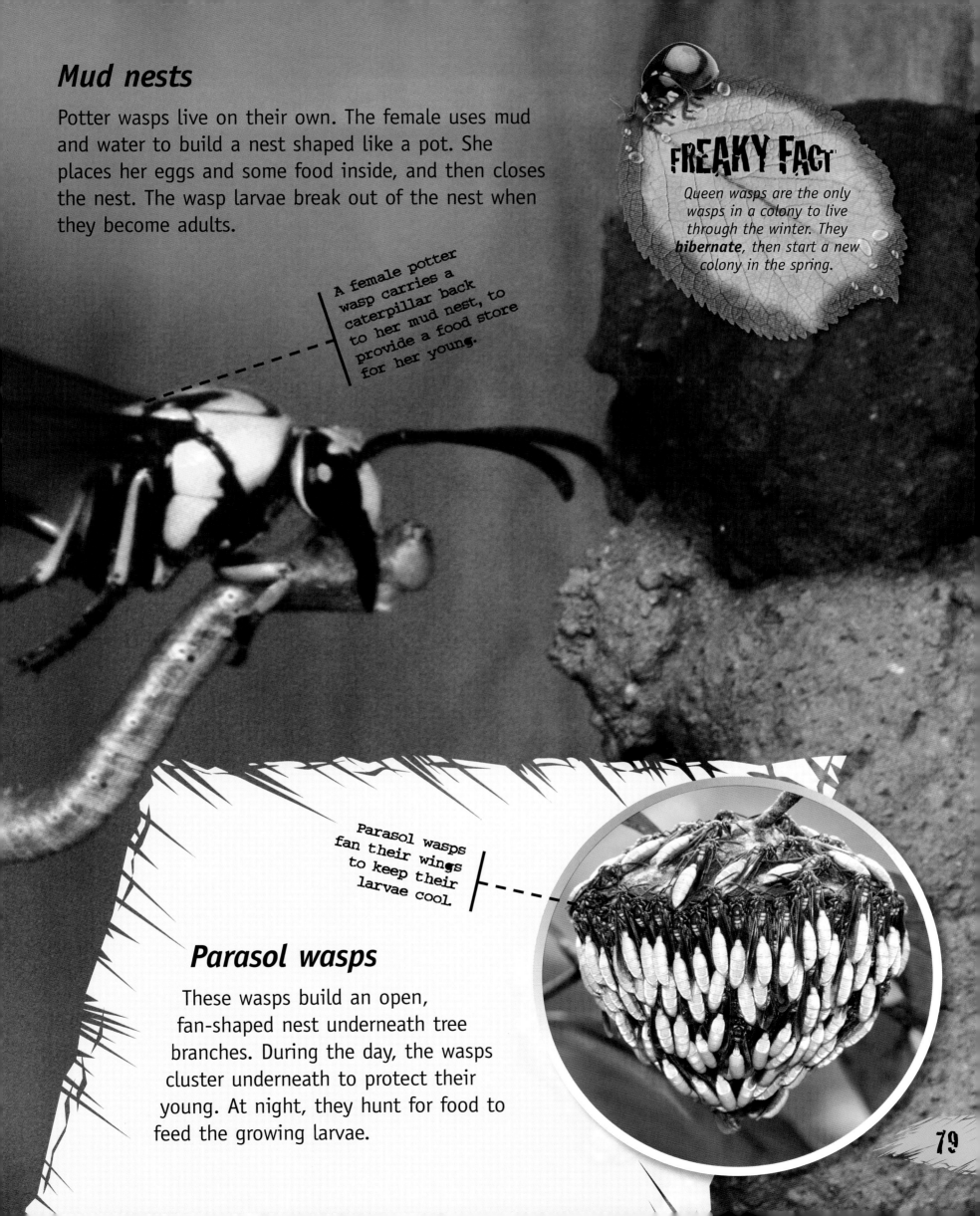

Mud nests

Potter wasps live on their own. The female uses mud and water to build a nest shaped like a pot. She places her eggs and some food inside, and then closes the nest. The wasp larvae break out of the nest when they become adults.

A female potter wasp carries a caterpillar back to her mud nest, to provide a food store for her young.

Parasol wasps fan their wings to keep their larvae cool

Parasol wasps

These wasps build an open, fan-shaped nest underneath tree branches. During the day, the wasps cluster underneath to protect their young. At night, they hunt for food to feed the growing larvae.

SAWFLIES, HORNTAILS, AND SABER WASPS

Sawflies are named for the sawlike egg-laying tube of the female. Horntails and parasitic wasps, such as saber wasps, have a similar tool. Adult sawflies and horntails look like wasps but do not have a narrow waist.

FREAKY FACT

The larvae of some types of sawfly "talk" to each other by making tapping noises with their tails.

A saber wasp makes a hole in a rotten pine log and lays her eggs on or in a larva inside the log. She can tell where the larva is from the smell of its droppings.

Saber wasp

The saber wasp is a type of parasitic wasp. The female lays her eggs in or on the larvae of other insects, such as horntails and beetles, which live inside rotten wood. When the saber wasp larvae hatch, they kill and eat the other larvae.

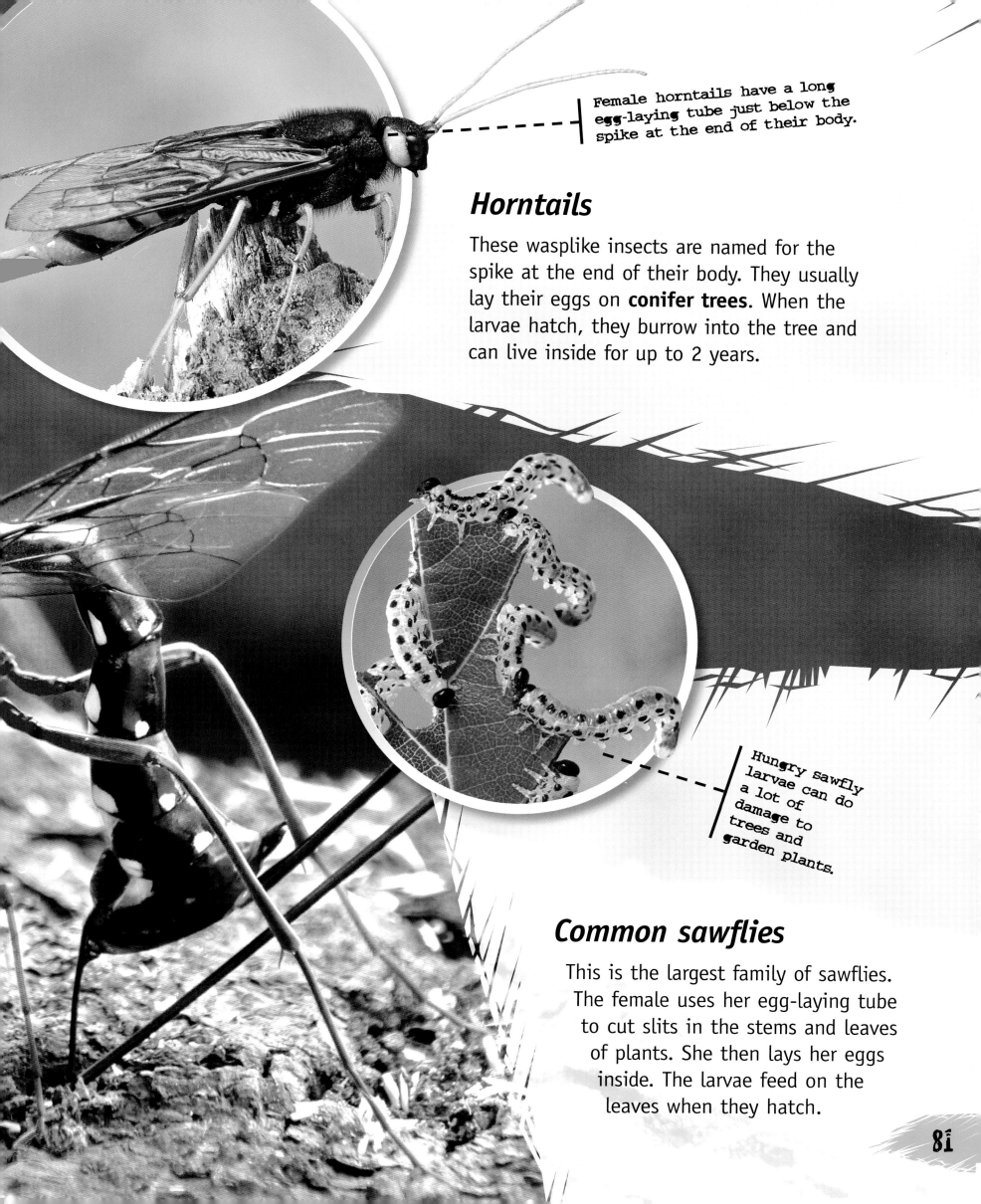

Female horntails have a long egg-laying tube just below the spike at the end of their body.

Horntails

These wasplike insects are named for the spike at the end of their body. They usually lay their eggs on **conifer trees**. When the larvae hatch, they burrow into the tree and can live inside for up to 2 years.

Hungry sawfly larvae can do a lot of damage to trees and garden plants.

Common sawflies

This is the largest family of sawflies. The female uses her egg-laying tube to cut slits in the stems and leaves of plants. She then lays her eggs inside. The larvae feed on the leaves when they hatch.

ANTS

Ants live together in colonies. There are often thousands of ants in one colony and at least one queen ant. The worker ants are female. They gather food, and look after the young.

Red ants

Like most ants, red ants like to eat sweet things. They feed mostly on **honeydew**, made by aphids. The ant strokes the aphid, and this makes it release the sugary liquid from its body.

FREAKY FACT

There are at least 10,000 different species of ant, and experts think there might be another 5,000 still to be discovered!

Many ants protect aphids from predators so they can keep feeding on their honeydew.

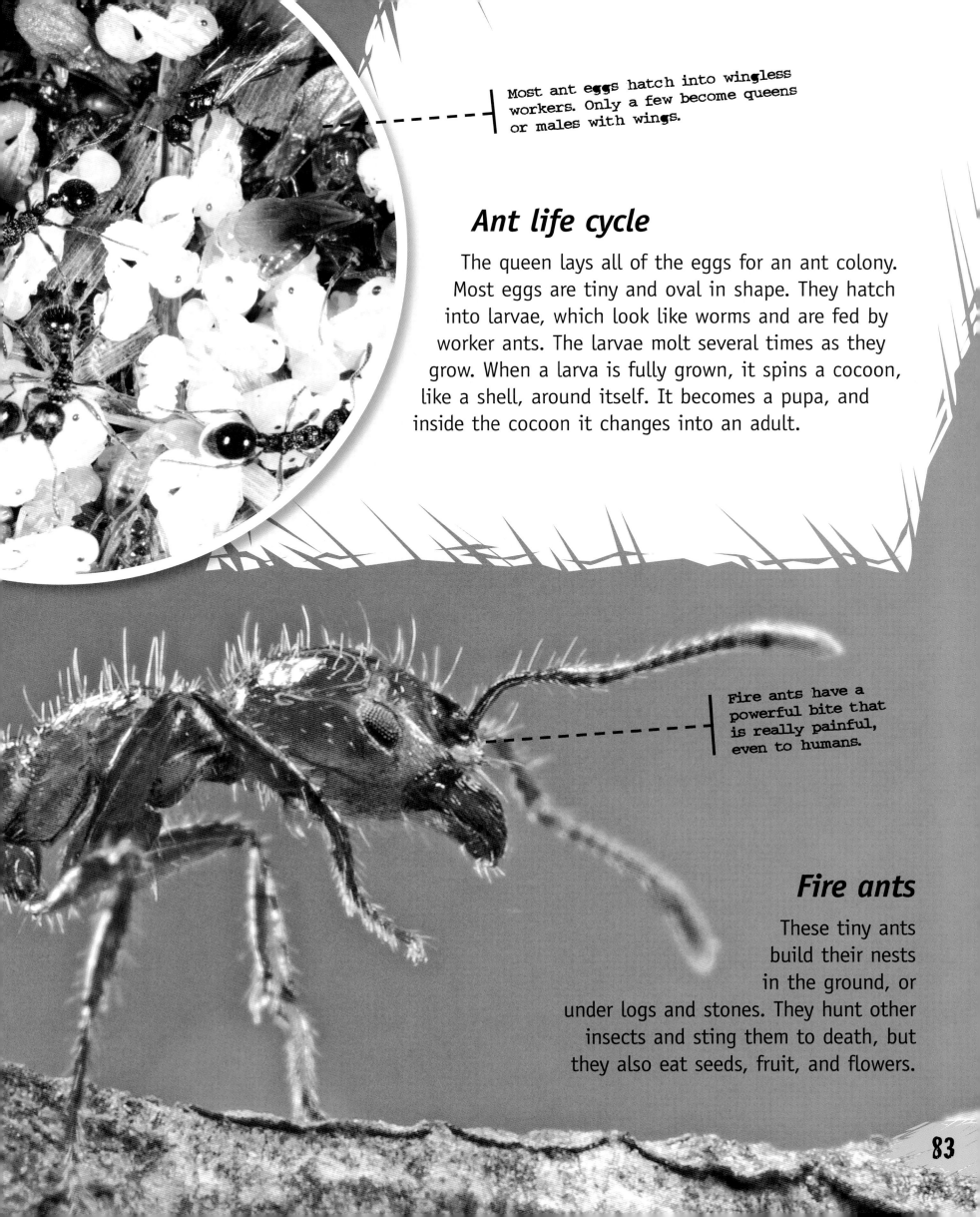

Most ant eggs hatch into wingless workers. Only a few become queens or males with wings.

Ant life cycle

The queen lays all of the eggs for an ant colony. Most eggs are tiny and oval in shape. They hatch into larvae, which look like worms and are fed by worker ants. The larvae molt several times as they grow. When a larva is fully grown, it spins a cocoon, like a shell, around itself. It becomes a pupa, and inside the cocoon it changes into an adult.

Fire ants have a powerful bite that is really painful, even to humans.

Fire ants

These tiny ants build their nests in the ground, or under logs and stones. They hunt other insects and sting them to death, but they also eat seeds, fruit, and flowers.

MORE ANTS

Different species of ants make different sorts of nests. Some ants build their nests underground, and others pile them up around tree stumps or logs. Army ants "camp out" in a different place each night.

These carpenter honeypot ants in Australia "throw up" nectar whenever a hungry ant demands to be fed.

Honeypot ants

Colonies of honeypot ants turn some of their workers into living storage jars! They feed these special ants with so much nectar and honeydew that their abdomen swells up like a balloon. When food outside the nest is hard to find, the swollen ants release the food for the other ants to eat.

Army ants

Army ants move in huge swarms during the day. At night, they camp under a log or in a hole in the ground. Sometimes, they simply link their bodies together to protect the queen and the larvae.

Army ants carry their eggs and larvae with them each day.

Sticky silk from a tiny larva joins leaves together as weaver ants build their nest.

Weaver ant

The weaver ant makes its nest from leaves. Some of the ants fold the leaves and others hold them in place. Then, another ant passes a silk-producing larva backward and forward between the edges of the leaves, like a spool of sewing thread, joining the leaf edges together.

85

LACEWINGS
AND ANTLIONS

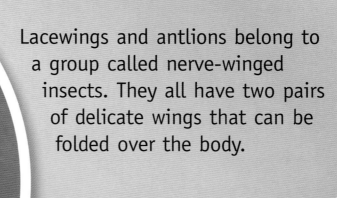

Green lacewings have tiny ears that pick up the sounds made by bats, and help them to avoid being caught.

Resting owlflies cling to twigs with their abdomen sticking out.

Lacewings and antlions belong to a group called nerve-winged insects. They all have two pairs of delicate wings that can be folded over the body.

Green lacewings

Green lacewings mostly fly at night, feeding on pollen, honeydew, and small insects. Lacewing larvae are fierce hunters with strong, gripping jaws. Some of them carry bits of plants on their back. This makes it easier for them to creep up on their prey without being noticed.

Antlions

Adult antlions look like dragonflies. The larvae are also known as doodlebugs. Some larvae dig a pit in sandy soil and lie in wait at the bottom. When passing insects step near the edge, they slip down into the pit, and into the antlion's waiting jaws.

An antlion larva hides at the bottom of its pit, waiting for prey to fall in.

FREAKY FACT

Lacewings attract a mate by shaking their abdomen. This makes a low, quiet noise, like a song.

Owlflies

Owlflies have bulging eyes and large antennae with "clubs" at the end. They are busiest in the evening, when they catch small insects as they fly around. Owlfly larvae live in trees or on the ground. Larvae that live on the ground often camouflage themselves with sand, making it harder for their prey to spot them.

87

DOBSONFLIES,
SNAKEFLIES, AND ALDERFLIES

Although these insects all have the word "fly" in their name, none of them is a true fly. Fossils show that they have been around for more than 250 million years.

Alderflies are not strong fliers, and stay close to the water where they grew up.

Alderflies

Alderfly larvae live in water for 2 or 3 years. They hide under stones and feed on small insects. When full grown, they leave the water. Adults live just long enough to mate and lay eggs.

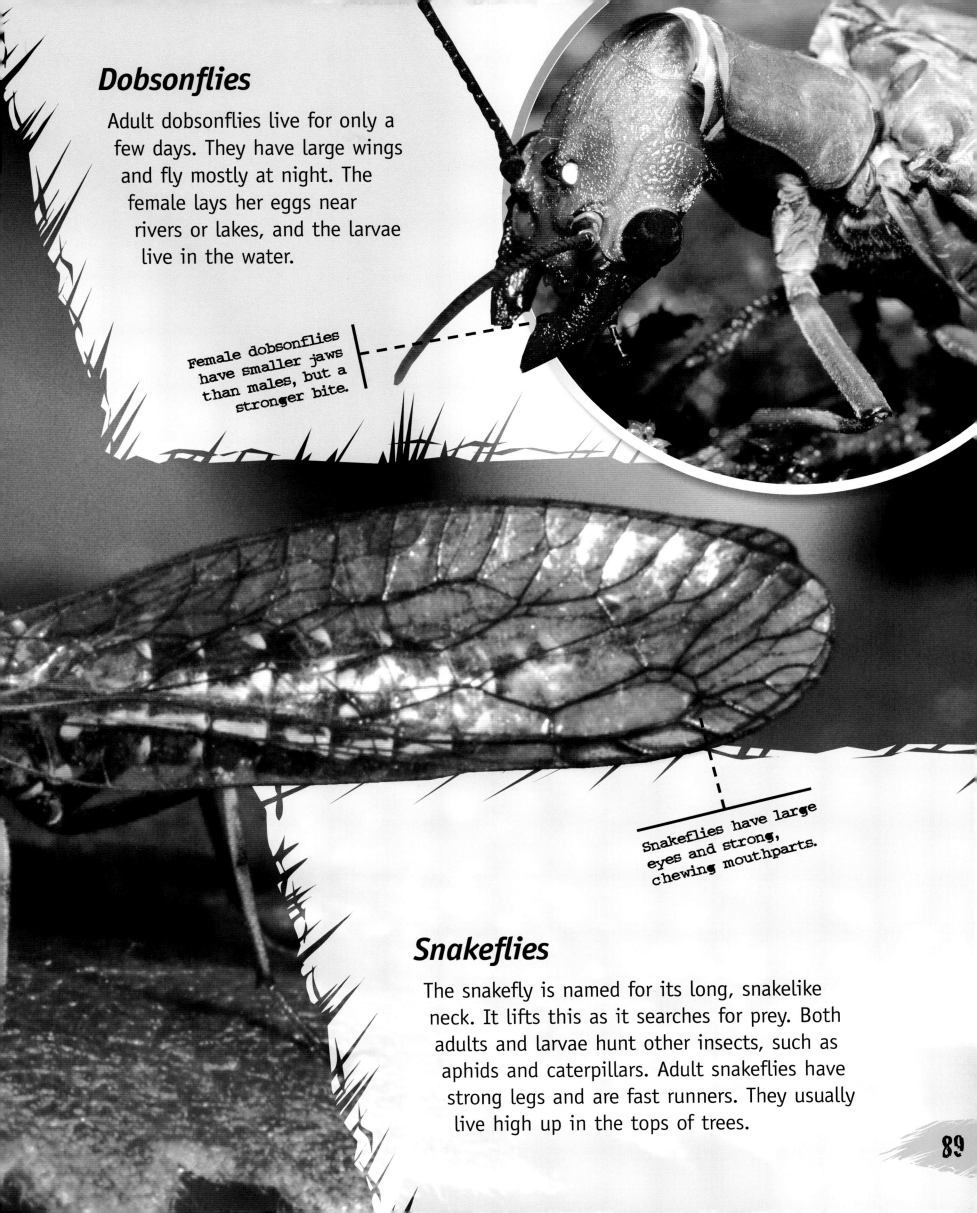

Dobsonflies

Adult dobsonflies live for only a few days. They have large wings and fly mostly at night. The female lays her eggs near rivers or lakes, and the larvae live in the water.

Female dobsonflies have smaller jaws than males, but a stronger bite.

Snakeflies have large eyes and strong, chewing mouthparts.

Snakeflies

The snakefly is named for its long, snakelike neck. It lifts this as it searches for prey. Both adults and larvae hunt other insects, such as aphids and caterpillars. Adult snakeflies have strong legs and are fast runners. They usually live high up in the tops of trees.

ATTACK AND DEFENSE

Insects have developed many different ways to protect themselves from predators. Lots of insects are also hunters. Some of them rely on speed or strength to catch their prey, and others use tricks and traps.

FREAKY FACT

Stick insects can break off a leg to help them escape from a predator. If they're young, the leg will grow back!

The bright colors on this saddleback caterpillar warn enemies that it is poisonous.

Spikes and bright colors

Some types of caterpillars have spiky bodies to put off attackers. Poisonous caterpillars are often brightly colored, which warns enemies to stay away.

The false eyes on this moth's wings have white centers, which make them look even more like real eyes.

False eyes

Some insects make themselves look bigger than they really are. They have large markings on their wings that look like eyes. The eye spots trick predators into thinking they've seen a much bigger creature that would be difficult to catch.

These army ants are working together to attack a tiger moth to feed their colony.

Strength in numbers

Some insects, such as ants, hunt in groups. Working together, they can catch much larger prey than they could on their own. They swarm all over a victim, such as a **millipede** or scorpion, and kill it with their bites.

91

FLIES, SCORPIONFLIES, AND FLEAS

There are more than 124,000 species of flies. After bees and wasps, flies are the most important **pollinators** of crops, and they also help to get rid of rotting waste. This chapter also looks at scorpionflies and fleas.

Maggots like to feed on rotting food. These maggots are eating a rotten peach.

Life cycle

House flies, and many other flies, have a four-stage life cycle. First the female lays her eggs. The larvae, known as maggots, hatch from the eggs after 8 to 20 hours. After 4 to 10 days, the maggots start the pupa stage of their life. They develop a reddish-brown skin, and inside this, they turn into a full-grown adult with wings.

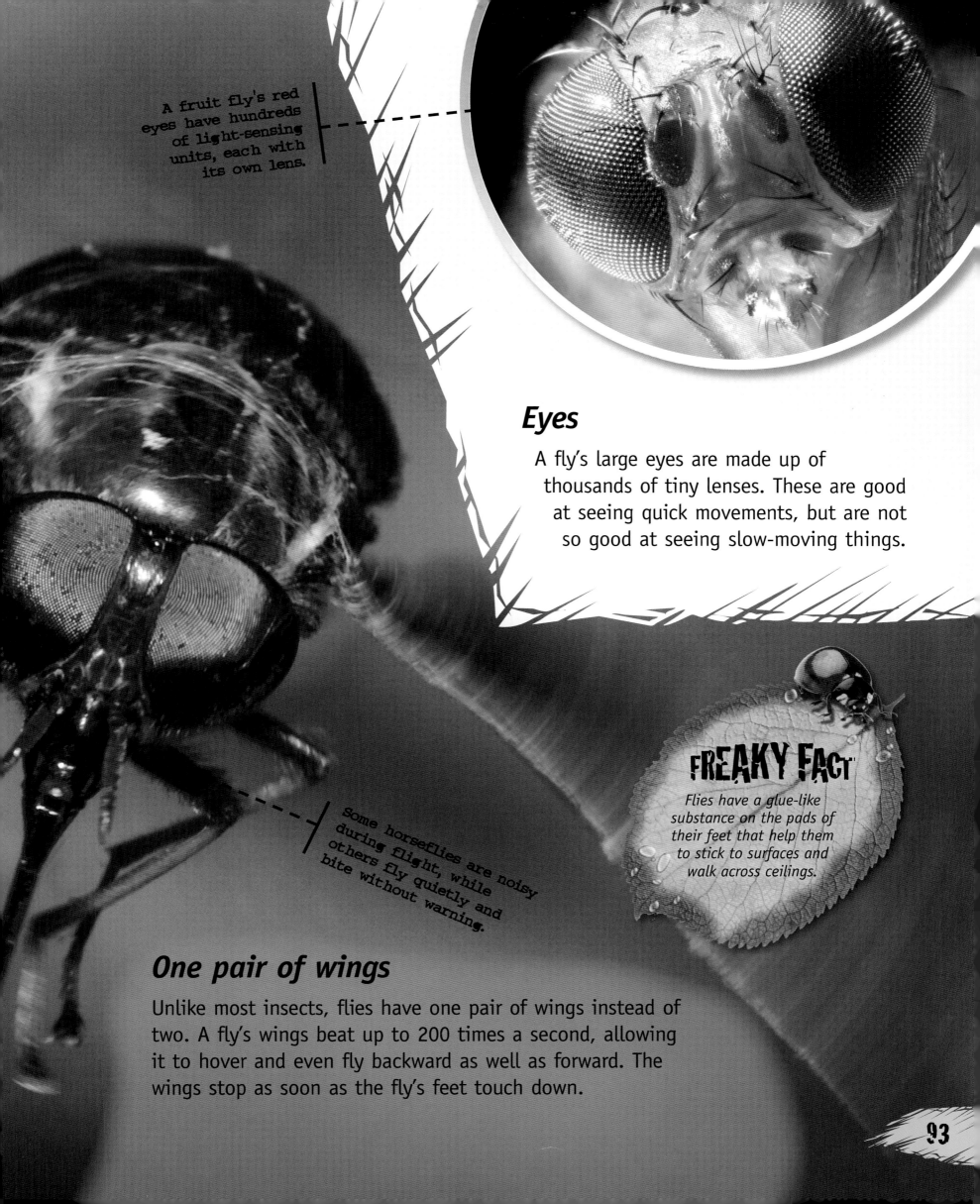

A fruit fly's red eyes have hundreds of light-sensing units, each with its own lens.

Eyes

A fly's large eyes are made up of thousands of tiny lenses. These are good at seeing quick movements, but are not so good at seeing slow-moving things.

Some horseflies are noisy during flight, while others fly quietly and bite without warning.

FREAKY FACT

Flies have a glue-like substance on the pads of their feet that help them to stick to surfaces and walk across ceilings.

One pair of wings

Unlike most insects, flies have one pair of wings instead of two. A fly's wings beat up to 200 times a second, allowing it to hover and even fly backward as well as forward. The wings stop as soon as the fly's feet touch down.

FLEAS
AND SCORPIONFLIES

Fleas and scorpionflies are not true flies. Fleas are tiny, wingless insects that feed on the blood of birds and other creatures. Scorpionflies belong to a separate group. They have large jaws and long, narrow wings.

Scorpionflies

Scorpionflies usually live in woodlands and forests, where they feed on dead insects. Sometimes they steal trapped prey from a spider's **web**. The female lays her eggs on the ground. When they hatch, the larvae also hunt for dead insects to eat.

FREAKY FACT

In the 14th century, rat fleas spread the Black Death, a disease that killed millions of people.

Scorpionflies are named for the curved end of the male's body, which looks like a scorpion's sting.

Oriental rat flea

This common flea lives on the blood of rats and humans, as well as other animals. It can spread disease if it bites a human after biting an infected rat.

A flea uses its mouthparts to bite, then suck up blood, and then spit into the bite.

A cat flea has spikes, like combs, on its head that help it to hold on to a cat's fur.

Cat flea

Although this flea usually lives on cats, it can also live on dogs. It has long, powerful back legs that help it to jump onto the animal to feed. Females lay their eggs in a cat's bedding, and the larvae eat waste from the adult fleas.

LONG-HORNED FLIES

The family of true flies is split into two groups: long-horned flies and short-horned flies. Long-horned flies usually have small bodies, long antennae, and long, thin legs.

A male mosquito uses its "stinger" to feed on nectar and plant sap.

Mosquitoes

You can usually hear a mosquito before you see it. Its wings beat so fast that it makes a whining noise as it flies. Most female mosquitoes bite animals with their long mouthparts, or "stinger," and suck their blood. In some countries, mosquitoes spread dangerous diseases.

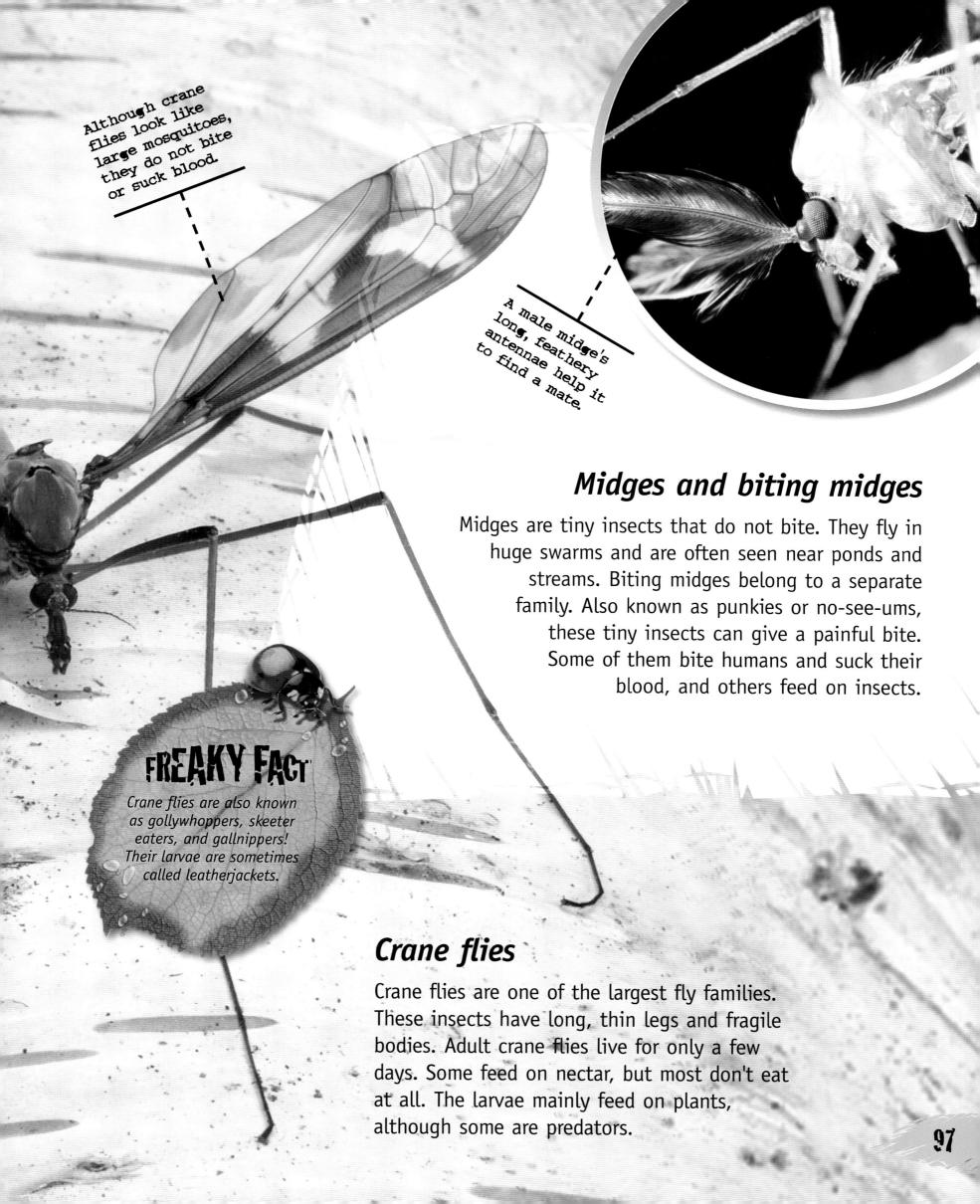

Although crane flies look like large mosquitoes, they do not bite or suck blood.

A male midge's long, feathery antennae help it to find a mate.

Midges and biting midges

Midges are tiny insects that do not bite. They fly in huge swarms and are often seen near ponds and streams. Biting midges belong to a separate family. Also known as punkies or no-see-ums, these tiny insects can give a painful bite. Some of them bite humans and suck their blood, and others feed on insects.

FREAKY FACT

Crane flies are also known as gollywhoppers, skeeter eaters, and gallnippers! Their larvae are sometimes called leatherjackets.

Crane flies

Crane flies are one of the largest fly families. These insects have long, thin legs and fragile bodies. Adult crane flies live for only a few days. Some feed on nectar, but most don't eat at all. The larvae mainly feed on plants, although some are predators.

SHORT-HORNED FLIES

Short-horned flies, such as horseflies, have bigger bodies and shorter antennae than long-horned flies.

Horseflies

Female horseflies feed on the blood of animals, including humans. They make a small cut on their victim, then lick up the blood that flows out. Their bites are painful, and the flies can carry diseases.

A tiny common bee fly adult feeds on a forget-me-not flower.

Male horseflies don't bite like the females. They feed on pollen, nectar, and tree sap.

Bee flies

These stout, hairy flies look like bees, and some also behave like bees. They hover in front of flowers, feeding on nectar by sucking it up with their mouthparts.

Robber flies have large eyes for spotting prey, and strong, bristly legs for catching hold of it.

FREAKY FACT

Bee fly larvae feed by sucking out the insides of other insect larvae.

Robber flies

There are about 5,500 species of robber fly. These fast-moving hunters chase and catch other insects in the air or on the ground. Once a robber fly has caught its victim, it uses its short, sharp mouthparts to suck out the liquid in the insect's body.

MORE SHORT-HORNED FLIES

Some short-horned flies feed and lay their eggs on dung and dead animals. They perform a useful job by recycling this rotting material.

Blow flies

Blow flies include blue bottles and green bottles, which have bodies that shine like polished metal. Adult blow flies feed on pollen and nectar, as well as anything that is rotting. Many species lay their eggs in dung, or in the bodies of dead animals, so the larvae can feed as soon as they hatch.

A housefly's long, strawlike mouthparts have a spongy "sucker" at the end

Blow fly females eat dung because it is full of protein, which they need to lay eggs.

Housefly

The housefly feeds on garbage and animal dung. It can eat only by mopping up liquid food. When it lands on something that it wants to eat, it spits on the food first. This helps to break it down, so the fly can soak it up.

Dung fly

The dung fly preys on other insects, including flies. The female lays her eggs on cattle dung, while the male guards the patch of dung from other males. When the larvae hatch, they feed on the dung.

FREAKY FACT

Female houseflies can lay up to 500 eggs in a few days. It takes less than 2 weeks for each one to become an adult fly.

A male yellow dung fly protects the female as she lays her eggs in fresh dung.

FLOWER, FRUIT, AND STALK-EYED FLIES

Some families of short-horned flies grow in a different way to the horseflies and their relatives. When the larva is full grown, it becomes a pupa. A pupa is a stage in between being a larva and an adult.

Fruit flies

Some fruit flies are serious pests that damage fruit trees and other crops. The females lay their eggs on plants or fruit, and when the larvae hatch, they burrow inside as they feed.

Male stalk-eyed flies usually have longer eye stalks than females.

Tiny fruit flies live on flowers and overripe fruit, such as apples.

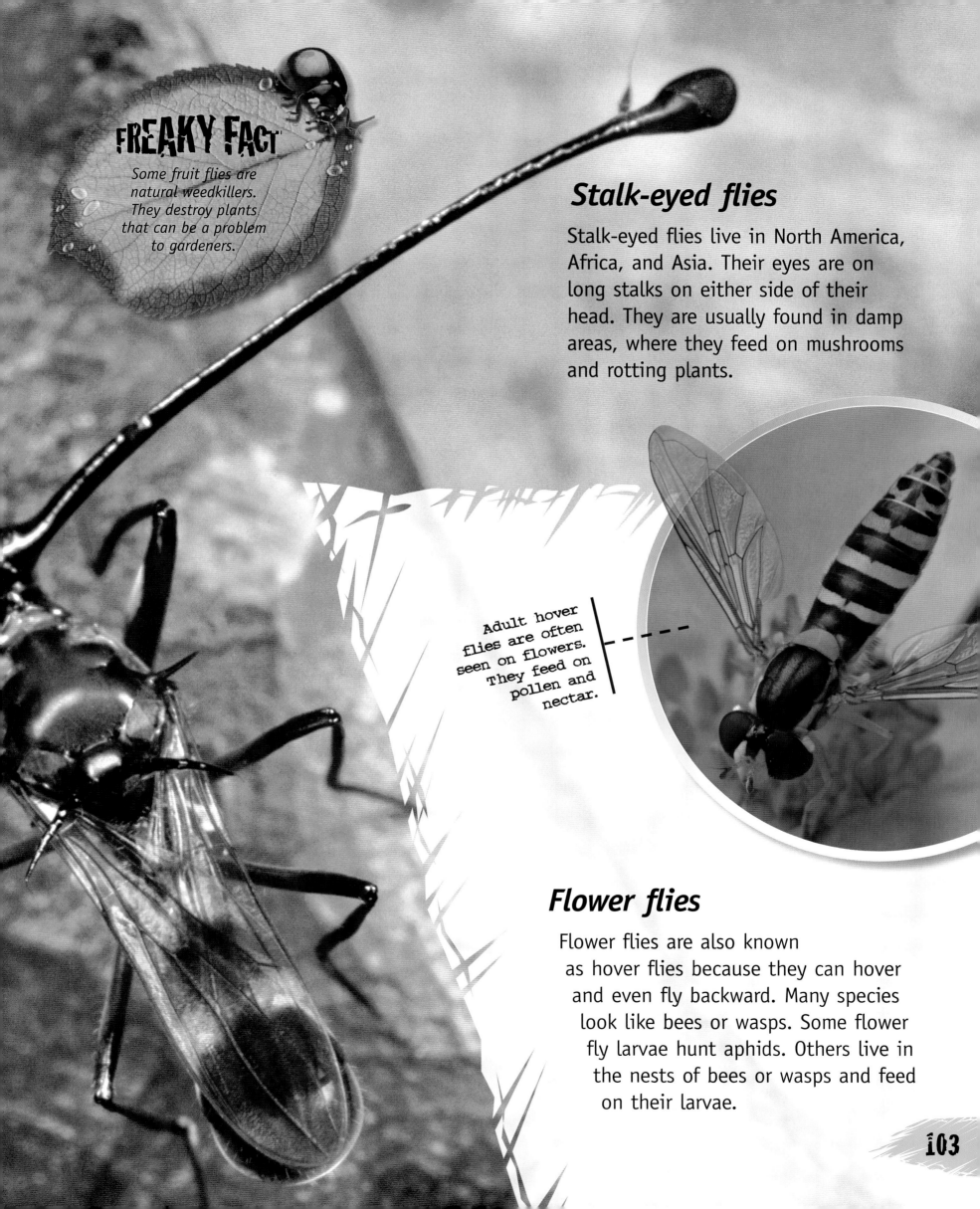

Stalk-eyed flies

Stalk-eyed flies live in North America, Africa, and Asia. Their eyes are on long stalks on either side of their head. They are usually found in damp areas, where they feed on mushrooms and rotting plants.

Adult hover flies are often seen on flowers. They feed on pollen and nectar.

Flower flies

Flower flies are also known as hover flies because they can hover and even fly backward. Many species look like bees or wasps. Some flower fly larvae hunt aphids. Others live in the nests of bees or wasps and feed on their larvae.

BUTTERFLIES, MOTHS, AND CADDISFLIES

Wherever plants grow, butterflies and moths can be found. They are the second-largest group of insects. This chapter also includes caddisflies, which look similar to moths but belong to a different insect group.

Eggs and caterpillars

Butterflies and moths have the same life cycle. The eggs are usually laid on plants. It takes from 1 to 3 weeks for the larvae, called caterpillars, to hatch.

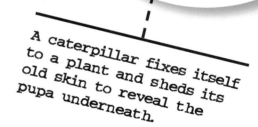

A caterpillar fixes itself to a plant and sheds its old skin to reveal the pupa underneath.

The pupa stage

When a caterpillar is full grown, it stops feeding and becomes a pupa, also called a chrysalis. Inside the pupa, the caterpillar grows antennae, wings, and legs.

Caterpillars, seen here hatching from their eggs, start to feed straight away.

After a butterfly leaves its chrysalis, it takes a few hours for its wings to harden so it can fly.

An adult emerges

Eventually, the pupa splits open and an adult moth or butterfly crawls out. Almost all butterflies and moths have two pairs of wings that are covered with tiny, overlapping scales. They all have antennae and sucking mouthparts for drinking liquid food.

FREAKY FACT

If disturbed, the blue morpho caterpillar secretes a fluid that smells of butter that has gone bad!

CADDISFLIES
AND MOTHS

Caddisflies look like moths, but have hairs on their wings instead of scales. There are about 11,000 species.

When resting, geometer moths spread their wings out flat.

Some caddisflies fix their cases so they stay in one place, and others move around with them.

Caddisflies

Most caddisflies live near water. Females lay their eggs in jelly on water plants. The eggs hatch into larvae that look like caterpillars. Underwater, the larvae live inside cases that they make from bits of leaf and twig joined with silk. The adults survive for only a few weeks and do not eat.

Geometer moths

This family of moths is one of the biggest of all moth families. The moths have narrow bodies and fragile wings.

Geometer caterpillars are also known as inchworms or loopers.

Geometer caterpillars

The name "geometer" comes from the Greek word "geo," meaning "earth," and "metron," which means "to measure." It refers to the way the caterpillars make a loop shape as they move along, like someone measuring with a tape measure.

FREAKY FACT

Some caterpillars escape from predators by spinning a line of silk. They use it to drop down from plants, like rappelling!

MOTHS

Although many moths are dull in color, many are brightly patterned. Like butterflies, moths have two pairs of wings covered in tiny scales (see page 12).

The bright markings on this tiger moth warn animals that it is poisonous to eat.

Tiger moths

Tiger moths have wide, hairy bodies and bold patterns on their wings. The caterpillars are known as woolly bears. They feed on plants that are poisonous to many animals, and store the poison to protect themselves against predators.

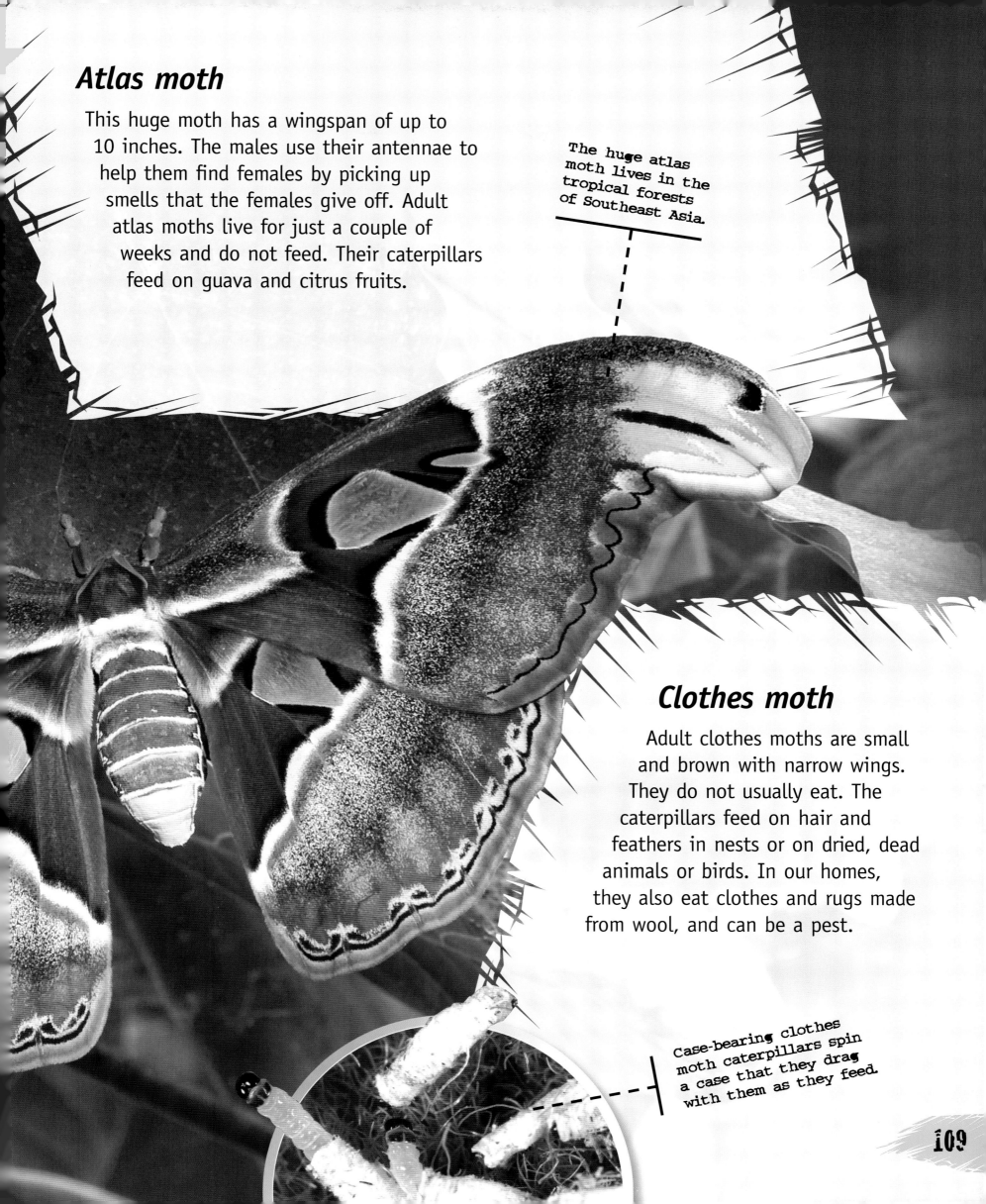

Atlas moth

This huge moth has a wingspan of up to 10 inches. The males use their antennae to help them find females by picking up smells that the females give off. Adult atlas moths live for just a couple of weeks and do not feed. Their caterpillars feed on guava and citrus fruits.

The huge atlas moth lives in the tropical forests of Southeast Asia.

Clothes moth

Adult clothes moths are small and brown with narrow wings. They do not usually eat. The caterpillars feed on hair and feathers in nests or on dried, dead animals or birds. In our homes, they also eat clothes and rugs made from wool, and can be a pest.

Case-bearing clothes moth caterpillars spin a case that they drag with them as they feed.

MORE MOTHS

Sphinx moths are also known as hawkmoths. Their wings beat so fast that they make a whirring noise as they fly or hover. Another family, the noctuid or owlet moths, is the largest of all moth families. It has more than 35,000 species.

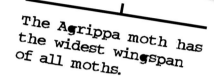

The Agrippa moth has the widest wingspan of all moths.

Agrippa or birdwing moth

The huge wings of the Agrippa or birdwing moth measure 12.5 inches across. This moth usually lives in forests, flies at night, and is also called the white witch! Most moths in the noctuid family are preyed on by bats. Many have special sense organs that hear the bats before they get too close.

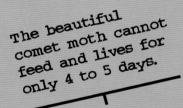

The beautiful comet moth cannot feed and lives for only 4 to 5 days.

Madagascar moon moth

The males of this moth, also called the comet moth, have a wingspan of nearly 8 inches. When the moon moth caterpillar is ready to become a pupa, it spins a silky cocoon full of holes. The holes stop it from drowning in the heavy rains of Madagascar.

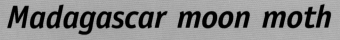

FREAKY FACT

Sphinx moths have the longest tongue of any moth. This helps them to drink nectar from deep inside flowers.

This sphinx moth is using its long tongue like a straw to feed on nectar from a thistle flower.

Sphinx moths

Like many moths, adult sphinx moths suck up nectar through their long, tube-shaped tongue. The tongue rolls up under the moth's head when it is not being used. Their antennae can pick up even the weakest flower scents, which helps them to find food at night.

BRUSH-FOOTED AND SWALLOWTAIL BUTTERFLIES

Monarchs and red admirals both belong to a family known as brush-footed butterflies. Swallowtail butterflies belong to a different family, and have tails on their back wings.

FREAKY FACT

Red admirals and monarchs have tufts of hair on the ends of their legs that look like tiny brushes!

Monarch

The monarch butterfly is a strong flier. Adults feed on the nectar of milkweed plants, and the caterpillars eat the leaves, which are poisonous. This doesn't hurt the monarch, but it does make the caterpillar and butterfly taste nasty.

The bright colors of the monarch caterpillar warn predators not to eat it.

King swallowtail

The tails on the back wings of the king swallowtail may help to distract its enemies and stop them attacking its head. It also has an organ behind its head that gives off a terrible smell to scare predators away.

King swallowtails live in the southern USA, Mexico, and northern South America.

In northern parts of the world, these fast-flying butterflies head south in winter to escape the cold

Red admiral

Adult red admirals feed on tree sap, juices from ripe fruit, and nectar. The caterpillars eat nettle leaves, and make themselves a shelter of leaves held together with silk.

MORE BUTTERFLIES

There are about 3,500 species of skipper butterfly. They get their name from the fast, skipping way they fly. Whites are another big family, with about 1,000 species. The gossamer-winged family is even bigger, with 6,000 species.

Silver-spotted skippers feed on nectar, usually from red, blue, or purple flowers.

Silver-spotted skipper

The silver-spotted skipper has a short, thick body like a moth's and hooks at the end of its antennae. The adults are often seen perching underneath leaves. Like moths, skippers stay hidden during the day, and come out to feed at night.

The small copper rests on plants with its wings half open, ready for a speedy take-off.

Cabbage white

The cabbage white has spread from Europe and Asia to North America, Australia, and New Zealand. The caterpillars are often thought of as pests. They eat plants from the cabbage family, such as cabbage, kale, and broccoli.

Female cabbage whites have two dark spots on each wing, and males have one.

Small copper

The small copper is a gossamer-winged butterfly. Its wings appear to shine like copper as it flies. The butterflies feed on nectar, and the caterpillars eat the leaves of plants such as dock and sorrel.

115

TRAVELING INSECTS

Many insects spend their whole lives on one plant, but a few, such as locusts and butterflies, can fly for hundreds of miles. They might travel to escape cold weather, find food, or build a colony somewhere new.

Insect journeys

Some insects make the same journey at the same time each year. This is called **migration**. It isn't only flying insects that **migrate**. Army ants walk for long distances, and owlet moth caterpillars march in groups to find new feeding places.

Army ants walk for long distances every day to find enough food for their colony.

Locust swarms

When food is hard to find or there isn't enough to go around, young locusts grow longer wings and set off in huge swarms across north Africa and the Middle East, looking for food. There can be millions of locusts in one swarm.

A swarm of locusts may spread over hundreds of square miles.

Monarch butterflies (background) gather in huge numbers in Mexico and feed (below) after their long journey.

Monarch migration

One of the longest of all insect migrations is made by the monarch butterfly. These butterflies cannot survive the cold winter in northern North America, so they fly south to California and Mexico for the winter. In spring, they return northward and lay their eggs on milkweed plants.

117

ALL ABOUT ARACHNIDS

Spiders, scorpions, and **mites** are not insects. They belong to a separate family, called arachnids. Arachnids have four pairs of legs, and do not have wings or antennae. There are at least 95,000 species, and they can be found all over the world.

The front section of a spider is protected by a tough plate called a carapace (say "ka-ruh-pace.")

Some species of scorpion have a sting that can be fatal to humans.

Scorpions

Scorpions are best-known for the dangerous sting at the end of their tail. When a scorpion attacks its prey, it swings its tail section forward over its body, so that it can drive the sting down into its victim.

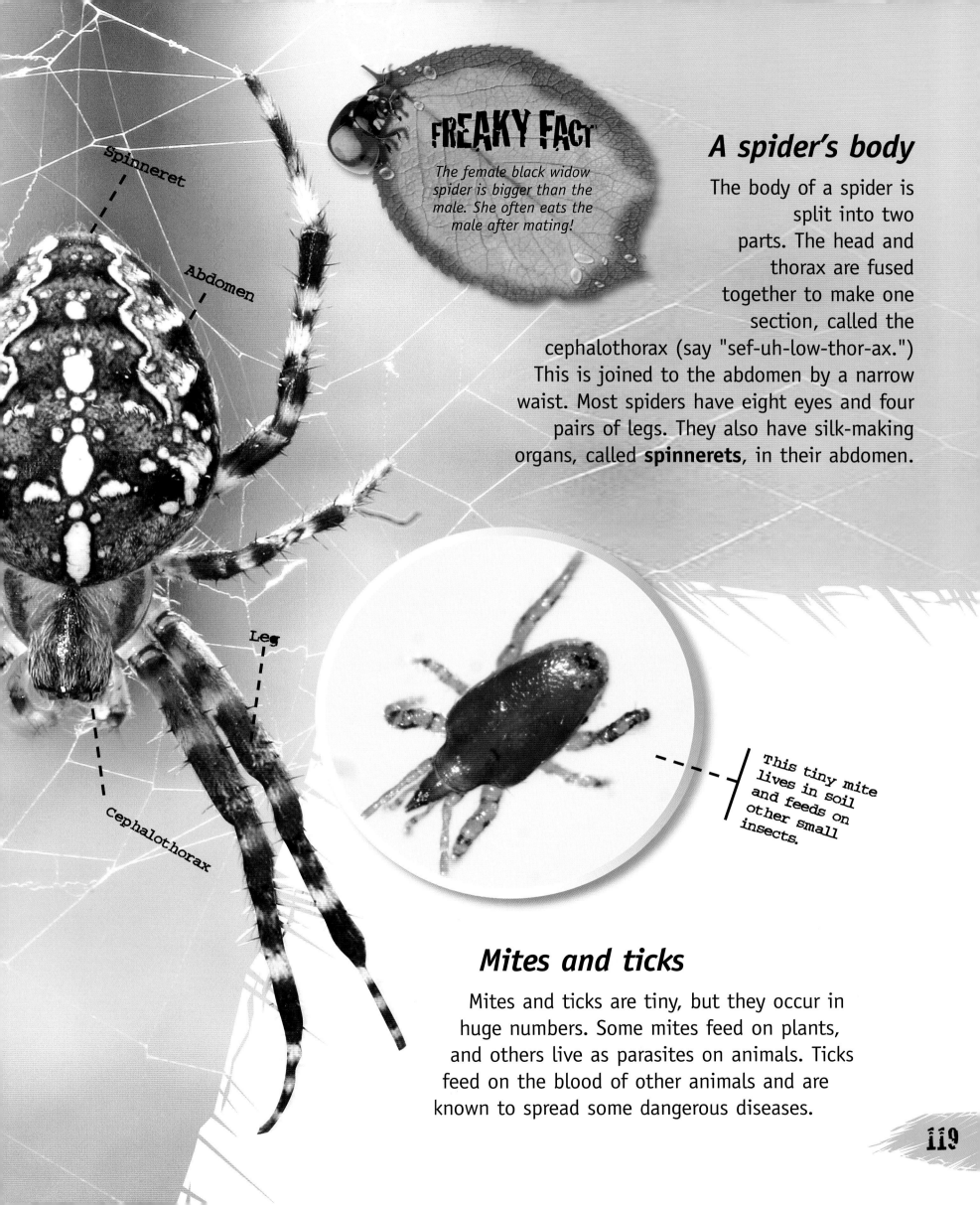

Spinneret

Abdomen

Leg

Cephalothorax

A spider's body

The body of a spider is split into two parts. The head and thorax are fused together to make one section, called the cephalothorax (say "sef-uh-low-thor-ax.") This is joined to the abdomen by a narrow waist. Most spiders have eight eyes and four pairs of legs. They also have silk-making organs, called **spinnerets**, in their abdomen.

This tiny mite lives in soil and feeds on other small insects.

Mites and ticks

Mites and ticks are tiny, but they occur in huge numbers. Some mites feed on plants, and others live as parasites on animals. Ticks feed on the blood of other animals and are known to spread some dangerous diseases.

SPIDERS

There are at least 40,000 known species of spider, and many more that have not yet been named.

Life cycle

A female spider lays her eggs and protects them by spinning an egg sac around them. Some spiders leave their egg sacs on plants. Others place them on a web or carry them around.

Deadly bite

When a spider bites its prey, poison flows through its **fangs** and paralyzes its victim, so it can't move. The poison dissolves the victim's insides, turning it into a liquid that the spider can suck up.

The strong jaws of a spider are armed with two large, curved fangs.

A mother spider guards her young, which are called spiderlings. They have just hatched and left their egg sac.

Eyes

Most spiders have four pairs of eyes. The pattern in which they are arranged varies from one family to another. The pair at the front forms the images, and in many spiders the other eyes just detect light. Jumping spiders have the best eyesight.

A jumping spider can swivel its large eyes.

FREAKY FACT

Nearly all spiders have a poisonous, or venomous, bite, but only a few are dangerous to humans.

TARANTULAS
AND RELATIVES

Tarantulas are some of the largest of all spiders. Most hide during the day and come out at night to hunt insects and small creatures, which they kill with a poisonous bite.

Trapdoor spiders

These spiders have an unusual way of catching prey. The spider uses a mixture of mud, spit, and silk to make a burrow with a hinged lid. It then sits inside the burrow and waits for prey. As soon as it feels something moving past the lid, it jumps out, grabs the prey, and takes it back inside its burrow to eat.

FREAKY FACT

Female tarantulas can live to be 30 or 40 years old! The males have much shorter lives of about 10 years.

An insect is caught after it touched a tripline near this trapdoor spider's burrow.

Goliath bird-eating spider

The Goliath bird-eating spider is the biggest spider in the world. It has a legspan of 12 inches! The spider does sometimes eat young birds (as its name suggests), but mostly feeds on insects, mice, snakes, frogs, and lizards.

The Goliath bird-eating spider lives in tropical rainforest in South America.

Females of this funnel-web tarantula from Bolivia are twice the size of the males.

Funnel-web tarantulas

Spiders in this family make a messy, funnel-shaped web that leads into a burrow. If a frog, lizard, or insect walks across the web, the spider rushes out to kill it.

SPITTING SPIDERS
AND RELATIVES

Some spiders spin webs to catch prey, and others spin them to protect their young. Some do not spin webs at all.

A female nursery web spider stands guard over her newly hatched spiderlings.

Nursery web spiders

The female nursery web spider makes a web to protect her young. She carries her egg sac with her, using her jaws, until the eggs are almost ready to hatch. Then, she spins a web over the egg sac to keep it safe while the **spiderlings** crawl out.

Spitting spiders

These spiders trap their prey by spitting strings of sticky liquid over them. As they move toward their prey, they turn their head from side to side so the sticky strings criss-cross over the victim's body.

FREAKY FACT

Young spiders use long strands of silk as parachutes to help them travel to new places. This is called ballooning.

A spitting spider sucks out the insides of its prey, which it has trapped with sticky strings.

Sheet-web weavers

These small spiders are sometimes called money spiders. They spin large, flat webs up to 12 inches wide. Lots of extra threads hold the web in place. When a flying insect hits one of these threads, it falls down onto the sheet web, where the spider is waiting.

A sheet web weaver lies in wait underneath its web, ready to grab its prey.

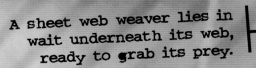

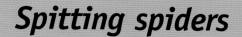

125

ORB WEB SPIDERS
AND RELATIVES

Orb-web, or orb-weaver, spiders are some of the best known of all spiders. They make the webs that we often see in parks and gardens.

FREAKY FACT

As soon as prey is caught in an orb-weaver's web, the spider rushes over and wraps it in strands of silk to stop it escaping.

An orb-weaver starts its web by making a non-sticky framework. Then it adds spokes and finally a sticky spiral for catching prey.

Garden orb weaver

Like other orb-weavers, garden orb-weavers spin two types of silk. One type hardens into a tough, non-sticky thread and is used to strengthen the web. The other is sticky and is used to catch prey.

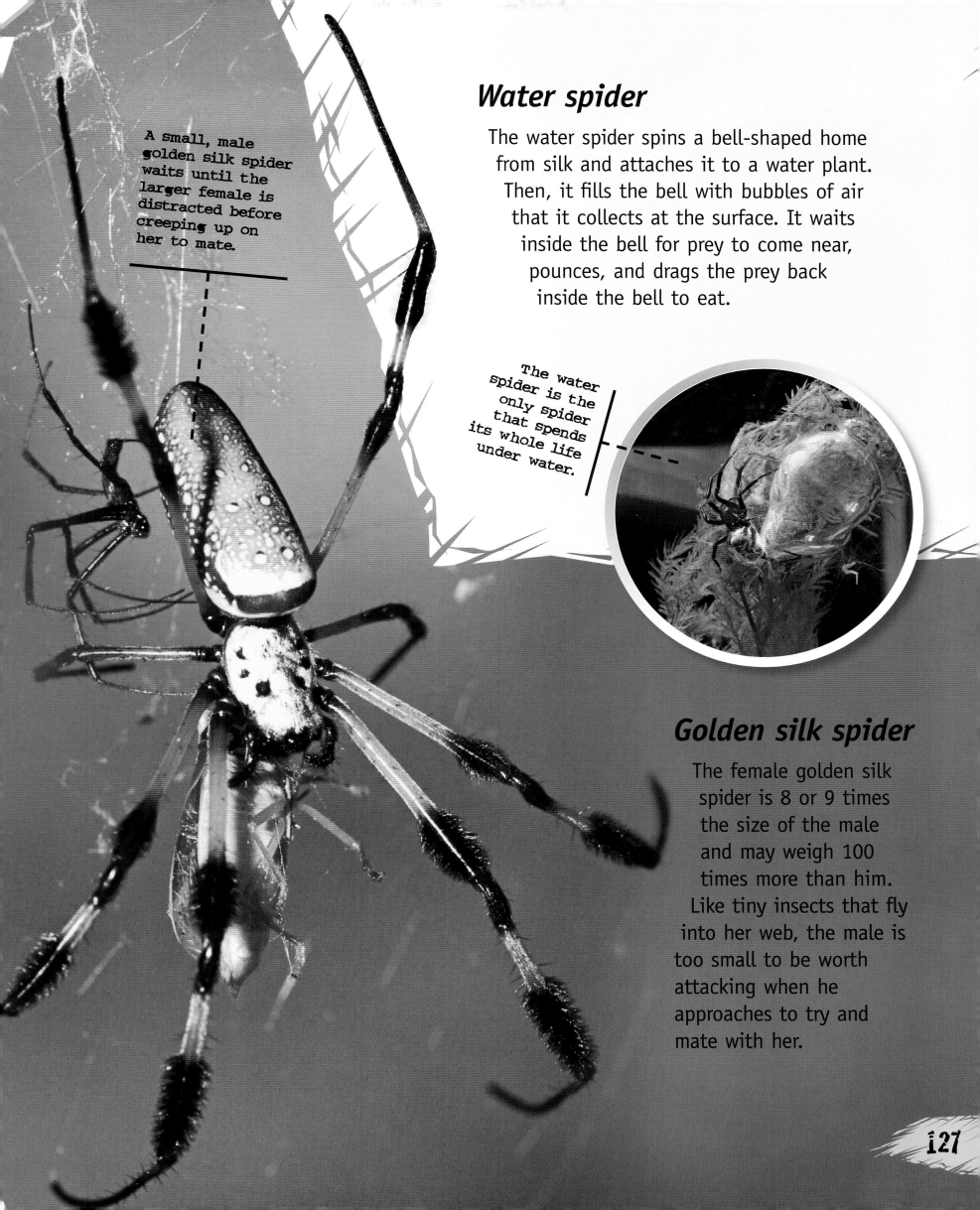

A small, male golden silk spider waits until the larger female is distracted before creeping up on her to mate.

Water spider

The water spider spins a bell-shaped home from silk and attaches it to a water plant. Then, it fills the bell with bubbles of air that it collects at the surface. It waits inside the bell for prey to come near, pounces, and drags the prey back inside the bell to eat.

The water spider is the only spider that spends its whole life under water.

Golden silk spider

The female golden silk spider is 8 or 9 times the size of the male and may weigh 100 times more than him. Like tiny insects that fly into her web, the male is too small to be worth attacking when he approaches to try and mate with her.

JUMPING SPIDERS
AND RELATIVES

Some spiders, such as jumping spiders and lynx spiders, have good eyesight and watch out for prey. Others rely more on their sense of touch. They sense movement through tiny hairs on their body and legs.

A jumping spider leaps onto its grasshopper prey, trailing a silk safety line.

Jumping spiders

Unlike many spiders, jumping spiders have good eyesight, and this helps them to find prey. Once they have spotted a victim, they pounce on it. However, before jumping, they fix a silk thread to the ground, so they can return along it safely to their hideout.

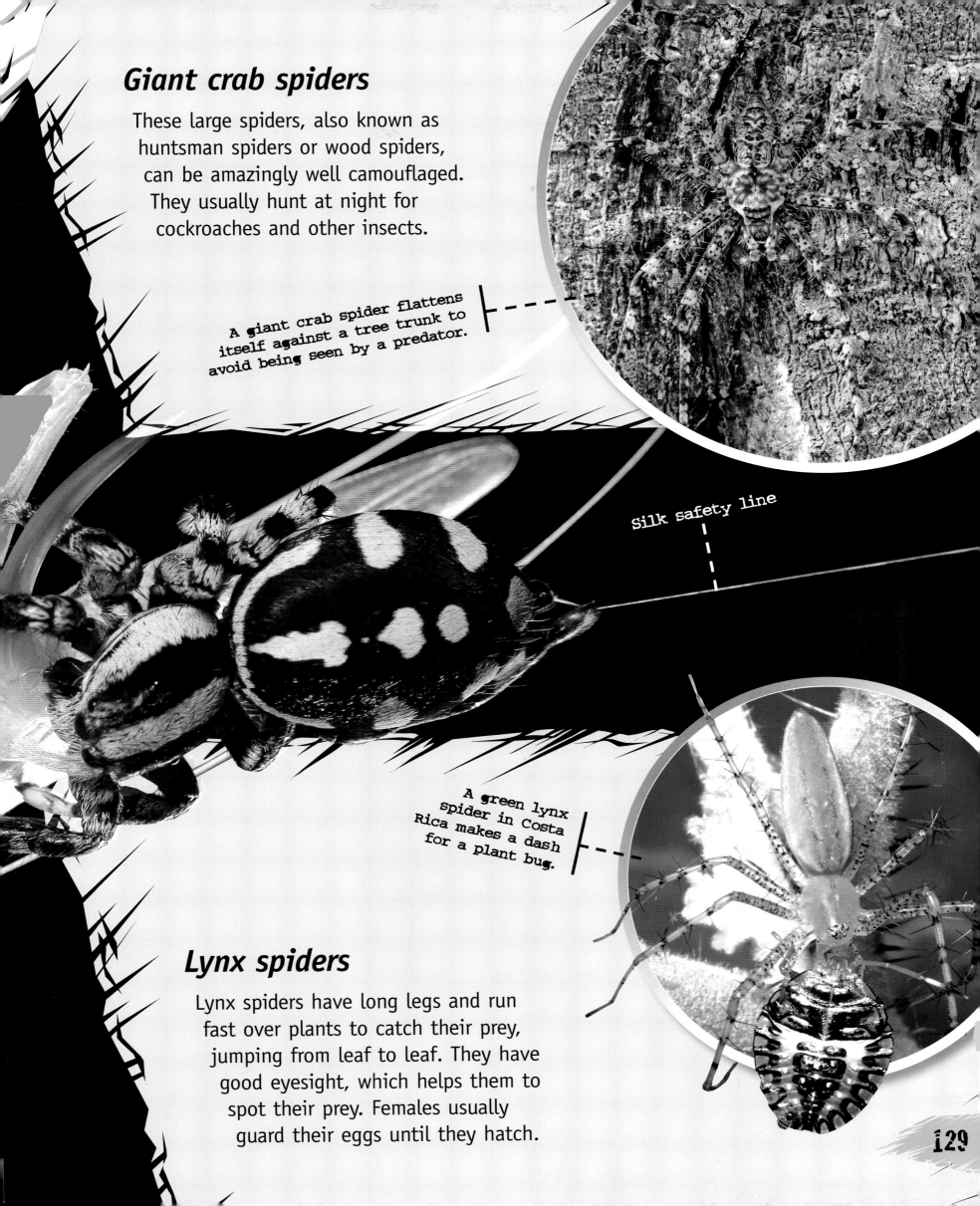

Giant crab spiders

These large spiders, also known as huntsman spiders or wood spiders, can be amazingly well camouflaged. They usually hunt at night for cockroaches and other insects.

A giant crab spider flattens itself against a tree trunk to avoid being seen by a predator.

Silk safety line

A green lynx spider in Costa Rica makes a dash for a plant bug.

Lynx spiders

Lynx spiders have long legs and run fast over plants to catch their prey, jumping from leaf to leaf. They have good eyesight, which helps them to spot their prey. Females usually guard their eggs until they hatch.

129

MITES AND TICKS

Mites and ticks are the smallest arachnids. They live almost everywhere, in hot and cold places and even in the sea. Ticks feed on the blood of animals.

Adult house mites are just 0.2 inches long.

House-dust mites

These tiny mites are common in houses all over the world. They feed on the tiny pieces of skin found in house dust. Their droppings can sometimes cause allergies and make people unwell.

Hard ticks

Hard ticks cling to plant stems and climb on to any animal that brushes past. The tick holds on to the animal with its strong mouthparts and feeds on its blood for 5 to 7 days. Some species spread diseases as they feed.

Female ticks can swell to many times their normal size as they drink an animal's blood.

Velvet mites are named for the thick, soft hair that covers their body.

Velvet mites

These mites are common in soil and moss, and on walls. Adult velvet mites feed mostly on insect eggs. Their larvae feed as parasites on insects and spiders.

SCORPIONS
AND RELATIVES

Most scorpions live in warm parts of the world. They use the poisonous sting at the end of their body to kill prey and protect themselves. Scorpions find prey using their sense of touch.

A female buthid scorpion carries her newly hatched young on her back until they can look after themselves.

Buthid scorpions

These large scorpions hide under stones during the day and come out at night to hunt. They grab insects and spiders in their powerful claws, or pincers. Then, they swing their sting forward over their body and stab the victim.

Wind scorpions

Wind scorpions, also known as sun scorpions, are common in deserts. These fast-running hunters come out at night to prey on insects or small lizards. They can grow up to 6 inches long, not including the legs!

A wind scorpion's large jaws can cut through skin and thin bones.

FREAKY FACT

Most other types of arachnid lay eggs, but scorpions give birth to live babies, known as scorplings.

Harvestmen

Sometimes known as daddy-long-legs, these arachnids have a round body and very long, thin legs. If they feel threatened, harvestmen may spray a bad-smelling liquid at their attacker.

Harvestmen usually come out at night to hunt for insects.

RECORD BREAKERS

Most insects and spiders are small, but a few grow to be surprisingly big. Some are super speedy, and others have amazing jumping skills. One of the most dangerous is the mosquito, because it carries and spreads diseases, such as **malaria**.

Giant weta are so heavy that they cannot jump. They live on islands near New Zealand.

Biggest and heaviest

The world's longest insect is Chan's megastick, a tropical stick insect from Borneo. It measures an incredible 22.3 inches long. The heaviest adult insect is a giant weta, weighing 2.5 ounces.

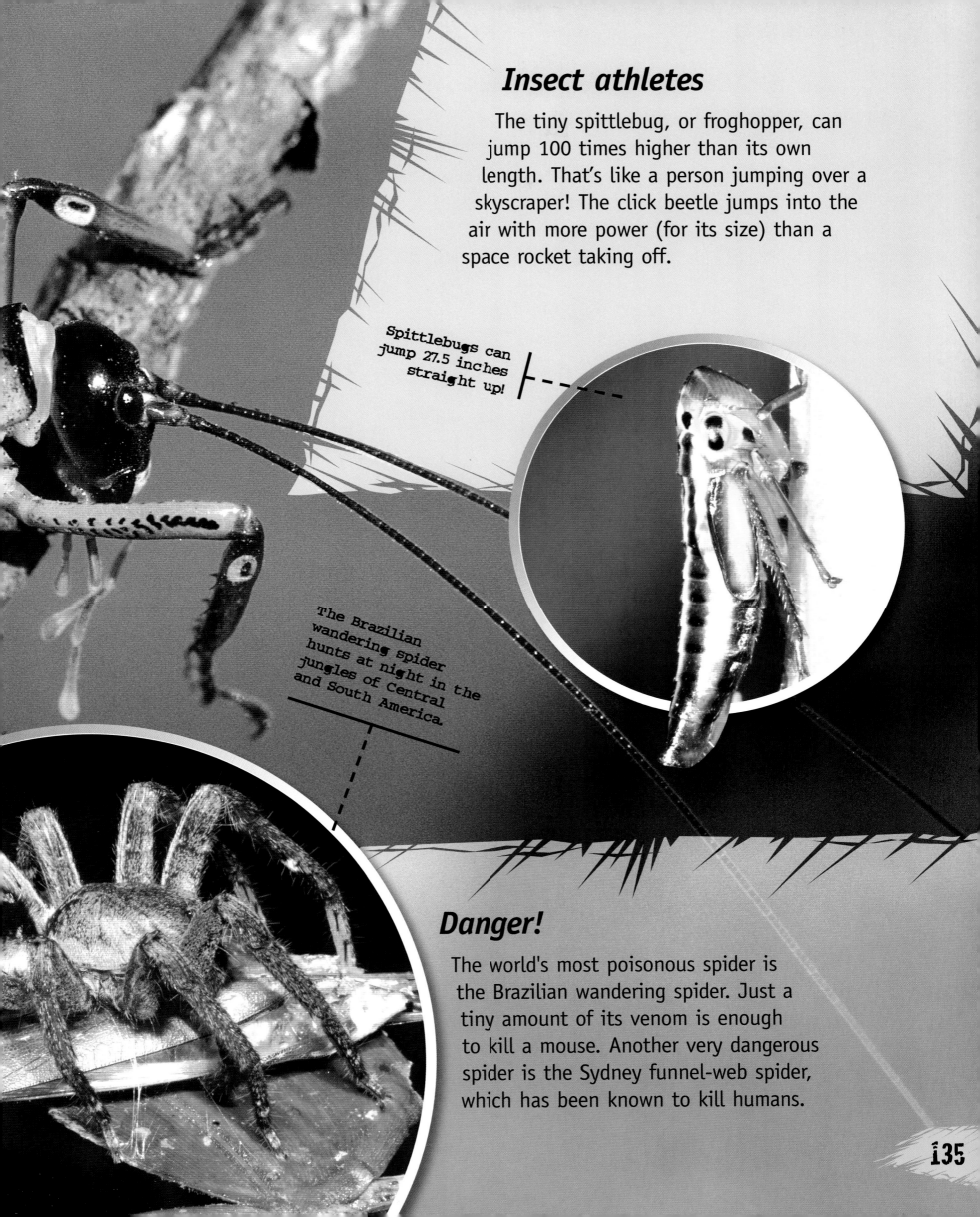

Insect athletes

The tiny spittlebug, or froghopper, can jump 100 times higher than its own length. That's like a person jumping over a skyscraper! The click beetle jumps into the air with more power (for its size) than a space rocket taking off.

Spittlebugs can jump 27.5 inches straight up!

The Brazilian wandering spider hunts at night in the jungles of Central and South America.

Danger!

The world's most poisonous spider is the Brazilian wandering spider. Just a tiny amount of its venom is enough to kill a mouse. Another very dangerous spider is the Sydney funnel-web spider, which has been known to kill humans.

GLOSSARY

Abdomen
back end of an insect's body, attached to the thorax

Adapting
changing over time to suit new conditions, such as a particular type of habitat

Antarctica
the continent around the South Pole, mostly covered by ice sheets

Antennae
two long, thin feelers on an insect's head that help the insect to smell, taste, and touch things around it

Aphids
tiny insects that feed by sucking nectar from plants

Arachnids
creatures with a 2-part body and 8 jointed legs. Spiders, scorpions, ticks, and mites are arachnids

Camouflage
the colors or patterns on an animal's body that help it to blend in with its surroundings so it cannot easily be seen by enemies or prey

Caterpillars
the larvae of moths and butterflies. Caterpillars may be brightly colored to warn predators they are poisonous, or camouflaged to blend in with the surrounding leaves

Cell
a very small, 6-sided "room" in the nest of a bee or wasp, used for storing food or eggs

Cocoon
a silky case spun by an insect larva to protect itself while it is a pupa (see Pupa). Also a case spun by a female spider to protect her eggs

Colony
a group of insects of the same species, living together in one place. Ants, termites, and some species of bees and wasps live in colonies.

Conifer trees
trees that produce cones and have evergreen needles

Crops
plants, such as wheat, corn, fruits, or vegetables, grown by farmers for people to eat

Disease
an illness that prevents the body from working normally

Drones
male bees. Their only job is to mate with the queen

Fangs
sharp, pointed mouthparts, used to inject venom

Fossils

the remains of prehistoric creatures hardened in rock or preserved in amber

Fungus

molds, mushrooms, and toadstools are types of fungus. They are not green plants and not animals

Glands

parts of the body that produce special substances, such as poisons

Habitats

the places where animals or plants live

Halteres

two tiny parts, or structures, behind a fly's wings that help the fly to balance while it is flying through the air

Hibernates

spends the winter sleeping to save energy

Honeydew

a sweet, sticky liquid produced by aphids and eaten by ants and ladybugs

Insects

animals with a head, thorax, abdomen, 3 pairs of legs attached to the thorax, and 1 or 2 pairs of wings

Invertebrates

animals that do not have a backbone. More than 95 percent of all animal species are invertebrates

Larva

an insect's young, after it has hatched from an egg and before it becomes an adult. A larva looks quite different from the adult insect. A caterpillar, for example, is the larva of a butterfly

Larvae

more than one larva

Malaria

a disease carried by mosquitoes that can be deadly to humans

Mate

one of a pair of animals that has chosen another to produce young. To come together to produce young

Mating

the coming together of male and female creatures to produce young

Migrate

to make a regular journey from one place to another

Migration

a journey made by an animal, often at the same time each year, to find food or a mate

Millipede

a creature with a long body made up of many segments, most of which have 2 pairs of legs. Some common species have up to 400 legs!

Mites

tiny creatures related to spiders and ticks

Molt

to shed, or cast off, a layer of skin ready for a new one to grow in its place

Nectar

the sugary liquid produced by many flowers that some insects suck up as food

GLOSSARY

Nymphs

the young or larval stage of some insects, such as grasshoppers. Nymphs usually look like the adults, but are smaller and do not have full-size wings

Organs

parts of the body that do a particular job. The heart is an organ that pumps blood, and bees have special organs that make wax

Paralyzes

makes it impossible for a creature to move all or part of its body

Parasites

animals or plants that live on other animals or plants. Parasites often harm the thing they live on

Pollen

a powder produced by the male part of a flower. Pollen makes the female part of a flower produce seeds. It is usually yellow in color. Bees collect pollen and feed it to their young

Pollinators

insects, such as bees or flies, that carry pollen from one flower to another, helping them to produce seeds

Predators

animals that hunt and kill other animals for food

Prey

an animal that is hunted and eaten by another animal

Pupa

a stage in the life cycle of some insects. During this stage, an insect changes from a larva into an adult

Queen

an egg-laying female in a colony of ants, bees, wasps, or termites

Rainforests

forests in tropical countries, such as Brazil, that get very heavy rainfall for much of the time. Rainforests are hotter and wetter than other forests, and are home to huge numbers of insects, other animals, and plants

Resin

a sticky substance that oozes from some trees, such as fir and pine trees

Sap

watery solution in the stems and trunks of plants

Silk

delicate threads made by spiders and some insects, such as silkworms. Also the fabric made from the cocoons of silkworms

Solitary

living alone, not as part of a group or colony

Species

a group of animals with similar characteristics. Animals of the same species can mate and produce young, which in turn are able to have young of their own

Spiderling

a newly hatched spider

Spinnerets

fine tubes at the end of a spider's abdomen. Silk for spinning a web comes out of the spider's body through the spinnerets.

Swarms

large groups of insects, such as bees, ants, or locusts, that travel together

Thorax

the part of an insect's body between the head and the abdomen. An insect's legs are attached to the thorax

Venom

A poisonous liquid made by an insect or arachnid. It is used to kill prey, or stop it from moving

Vibrations

small, fast movements to and fro, as when you twang a piece of elastic

Web

fine, silky threads, woven by a spider. Some webs are made to trap prey and others are made to protect spiderlings

Wing cases

a beetle's hard front wings, which cover and protect the thin back wings when they are closed

Wingspan

the distance from the tip of one wing to the tip of the other wing when the wings are open, or spread out

Workers

the insects in a colony that build the nest, find food, and care for young

INDEX

INDEX

PICTURE CREDITS

1 Murray Cooper/Minden Pictures; 2-3 Michael Durham/Minden Pictures; 4-5 Konrad Wothe/Minden Pictures; 6b Sh/ © Henrik Larsson; 6-7 Sh/ © Herbert Kratky; 7tr Wendy Dennis; 8br Sh/ © Sofiaworld; 8-9 Matt Cole; 9t Martin B Withers; 10bl Emanuele Biggi; 10-11 Sh/ © Subbotina Anna; 11tr Sh/ © Marcel Jancovic; 12bl Sh/ © D. Kucharski & K. Kucharska; 12-13 Sh/ © Symbiot; 13tr Mitsuhiko Imamori/Minden Pictures; 14l Rene Krekels/Minden Pictures; 14-15 Robert Seitz/Imagebroker; 15r S & D & K Maslowski; 16t Justus de Cuveland/Imagebroker; 16b Richard Becker; 16-17 Andrew Bailey; 18l ImageBroker/Imagebroker; 18-19 Sh/ © James K. Troxell; 19tr Sh/ © Laurie L. Snidow; 20-21 Matt Cole; 21tr B. Borrell Casals; 22br Thomas Marent/Minden Pictures; 22-23 Paul Hobson; 23tr Rene Krekels/FN/Minden; 24tr Michael Durham/Minden Pictures; 24-25 Alfred Schauhuber/Imagebroker; 25tr Mitsuhiko Imamori/Minden Pictures; 26-27 © Biosphoto, Thierry Montford/Biosphoto; 27tl pd; 27r Sh/ © Doug Lemke; 28l Piotr Naskrecki/Minden Pictures; 28-29 Mitsuhiko Imamori/Minden Pictures; 29r Nigel Cattlin; 30br Nigel Cattlin; 30-31 Martin B Withers; 31tl Hans Lang/Imagebroker; 32l Sh/ © Frank B Yuwono; 32-33 Bill Coster; 34 Albert Visage; 34-35 ImageBroker/Imagebroker; 35r Krystyna Szulecka; 36br Mitsuhiko Imamori/Minden Pictures; 36-37 Sh/ © sydeen; 37c Wendy Dennis; 38br Chien Lee/Minden Pictures; 38-39 Sh/ Redchanka; 40-41 Michael Durham/Minden Pictures; 41br Sh/ © kurt_G; 42-43 Sh/ © Wong Hock weng; 43tl Nigel Cattlin; 44bl Dave Pressland; 44-45 Sh/ © Steve Heap; 45tr Pete Oxford/Minden Pictures; 46l Nigel Cattlin; 46-47 Albert Lleal/Minden Pictures; 47r Jan Van Arkel/FN/Minden; 48br Foto Natura Stock; 48-49 Ingo Arndt/Minden Pictures; 49tl Mike Lane; 50-51t Thomas Marent/Minden Pictures; 50-51b Ingo Arndt/Minden Pictures; 52tr Murray Cooper/Minden Pictures; 52-53 Imagebroker, Michael Krabs,Imag/Imagebroker; 53br Imagebroker, Christian HÃ¼TTER; 54br Nigel Cattlin; 54-55 Konrad Wothe/Minden Pictures; 55br Nigel Cattlin; 56 Jef Meul/FN/Minden; 56-57 Piotr Naskrecki/Minden Pictures; 57br Jef Meul/FN/Minden; 58bl Nigel Cattlin; 58-59 Chien Lee/Minden Pictures; 59tl Chris Mattison; 60-61 Cyril Ruoso/Minden Pictures; 61tl Piotr Naskrecki/Minden Pictures; 61br Mike Amphlett; 62bl Imagebroker; 62-63 Richard Becker; 63cr Hans Lang/Imagebroker; 64l Mitsuhiko Imamori/Minden Pictures; 64-65 Murray Cooper/Minden Pictures; 65cr Mark Moffett/Minden Pictures; 66-67t Sh/ © Florian Andronache; 66-67b Emanuele Biggi; 67cr Mark Moffett/Minden Pictures; 68c Michael & Patricia Fogden; 69tl Mitsuhiko Imamori/Minden Pictures; 69b Robert Canis; 70-71 Bill Coster; 71tl Sh/ © SweetCrisis; 71br Imagebroker, Christian HÃ¼TTER; 72tr Jeremy Early; 72-73b Matt Cole; 73 Mitsuhiko Imamori/Minden Pictures; 74l Photo Researchers; 74-75 David Hosking; 75r Gary K Smith; 76-77 Matt Cole; 77tl Robin Chittenden; 77cr Richard Becker; 78l Alfred & Annaliese T/Imagebroker; 78-79 T S Zylva; 79br Pete Oxford/Minden Pictures; 80-81 Gianpiero Ferrari; 81tl Derek Middleton; 81c Thomas Marent/Minden Pictures; 82bl Nigel Cattlin; 82-83t Richard Becker; 82-83b Michael Durham/Minden Pictures; 84l Mitsuhiko Imamori/Minden Pictures; 84-85 Gerry Ellis/Minden Pictures; 85r Chien Lee/Minden Pictures; 86l Rene Krekels/Minden Pictures; 86-87 Martin B Withers; 87tr Robert Henno/Biosphoto; 88l Richard Becker; 88-89 ImageBroker/Imagebroker; 89tr Pete Oxford/Minden Pictures; 90-91 Rolf Nussbaumer/Imagebroker; 91t Cyril Ruoso/Minden Pictures; 91bl Mark Moffett/Minden Pictures; 92l Nigel Cattlin; 92-93 Murray Cooper/Minden Pictures; 93tr Michael Durham/Minden Pictures; 94-95 Matt Cole; 95tl pd (Centers for Disease Control and Prevention's Public Health Image Library); 95br Â© Biosphoto , Christian Gautier/Biosphoto; 96c Mark Moffett/Minden Pictures; 96-97 Derek Middleton; 97tr Jef Meul/FN/Minden; 98bl Roger Tidman; 98tr Martin B Withers; 99 Chien Lee/Minden Pictures; 100bl Erica Olsen; 100-101 Nigel Cattlin; 101br Richard Becker; 102b Jan Van Der Knokke/FN/Minden; 102-103 Mark Moffett/Minden Pictures; 103r Matt Cole; 104bl © Biosphoto , Yves Lanceau/Biosphoto; 104tr Richard Becker; 105 Malcolm Schuyl; 106l B. Borrell Casals; 106-107 Dave Pressland; 107tr Sh/ © Tyler Fox; 108l Robin Chittenden; 108-109 Konrad Wothe/Minden Pictures; 109b Nigel Cattlin; 110-111t S & D & K Maslowski; 110-111b Malcolm Schuyl; 111tl Imagebroker, Thorsetn Negro; 112bl FLPA; 112-113 Murray Cooper/Minden Pictures; 113r Silvia Reiche/Minden Pictures; 114l Sh/ © Steve Byland; 114-115 Kurt Möbus/Imagebroker; 115r Hugh Clark; 116br Christian Ziegler/Minden Pictures; 116-117 Fritz Polking; 117tr Piotr Naskrecki/Minden Pictures; 117b Sh/ © James Laurie; 118l Frans Lanting; 118-119 ImageBroker/Imagebroker; 119c Nigel Cattlin; 120bl Emanuele Biggi; 120-121 ImageBroker/Imagebroker; 121tl Matt Cole; 122b Photo Researchers; 122-123 Pete Oxford/Minden Pictures; 124bl Roger Tidman; 124-125 Piotr Naskrecki/Minden Pictures; 125br Peggy Heard; 126bl FLPA; 126-127 Photo Researchers; 127r Eiichi Shinkai/Minden Pictures; 128-129 Mark Moffett/Minden Pictures; 129tr Thomas Marent/Minden Pictures; 129br Michael & Patricia Fogden/Minden Pictures; 130l Nigel Cattlin; 130-131 Mark Moffett/Minden Pictures; 131r Dietmar Nill/Minden Pictures; 132-133 Claus Meyer/Minden Pictures; 133tl Mark Moffett/Minden Pictures; 133br Sh/ © Joseph Scott Photography; 134-135 (main) Ingrid Visser/Minden Pictures; 134-135b Photo Researchers; 135cr Dave Pressland.